There Is Always Room for One More Blessing

Septimus Barrock

ISBN: 979-8-89175-038-8 (sc)
ISBN: 979-8-89175-039-5 (ebk)

Acknowledgements

"I would like to acknowledge Shelly-Anne Samuel for supporting me on this project from the beginning, and for graciously making the pictures available for inclusion in the book." - Septimus Barrock

*"No matter how overwhelming darkness may seem,
it has no permanent ability to prevent the light
from making its presence known." - S. Barrock*

Waiting on God might feel like
a heavy weight on one's soul at
times, but wait He will show
up when you least expect it.

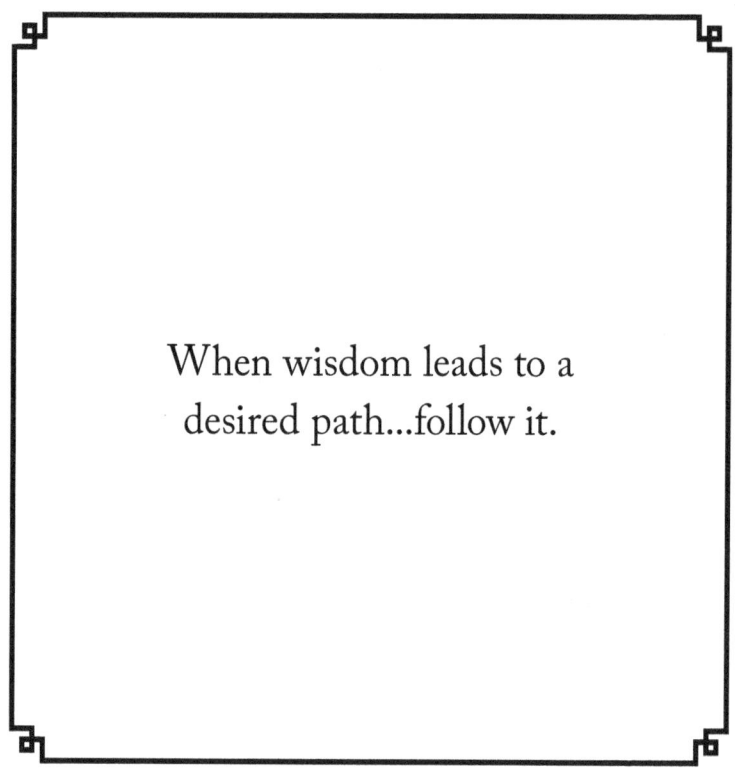

When wisdom leads to a
desired path...follow it.

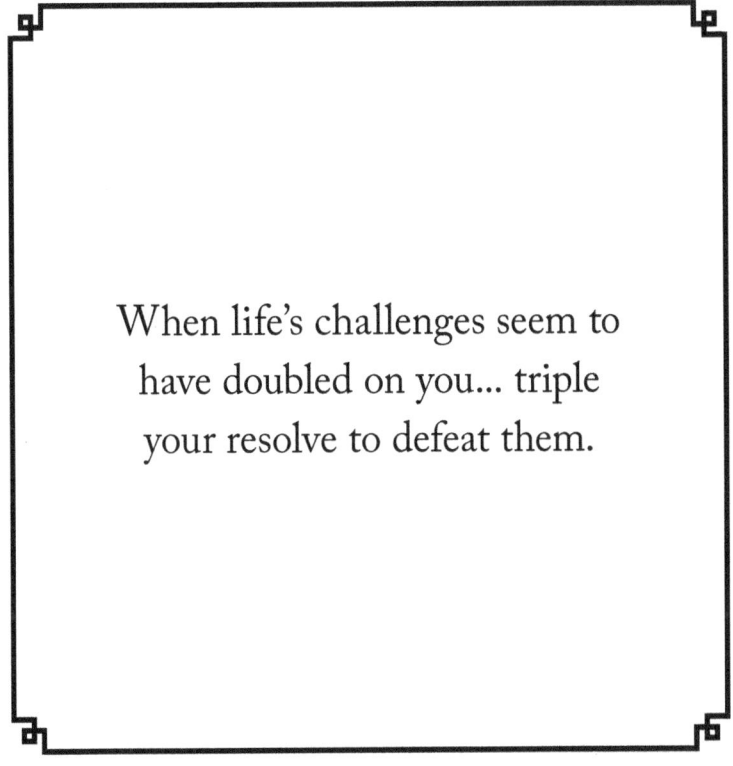

When life's challenges seem to have doubled on you... triple your resolve to defeat them.

Love recharges spirits...
show some today.

If one lets his light go dim, his world will no longer be lit.

Time does not run out on ideas, but time could run out before implementation.

Don't let the past control you...
don't let the bad times win.

Every act... good or bad... performed by a person is an investment in his future.

Choose something to
celebrate today.

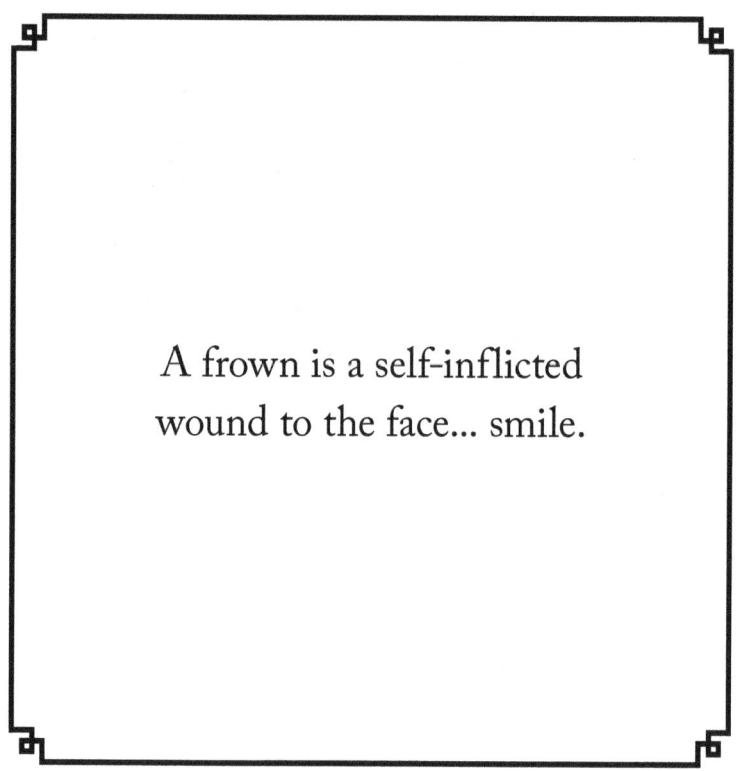

A frown is a self-inflicted
wound to the face... smile.

Endeavor to do all things well.

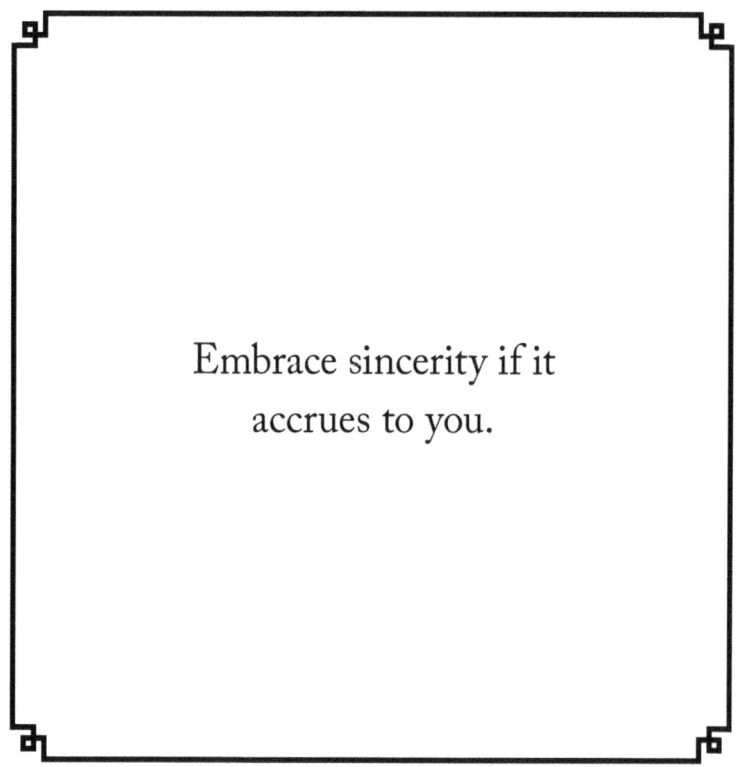

Embrace sincerity if it
accrues to you.

Get on board and stay
on board with life.

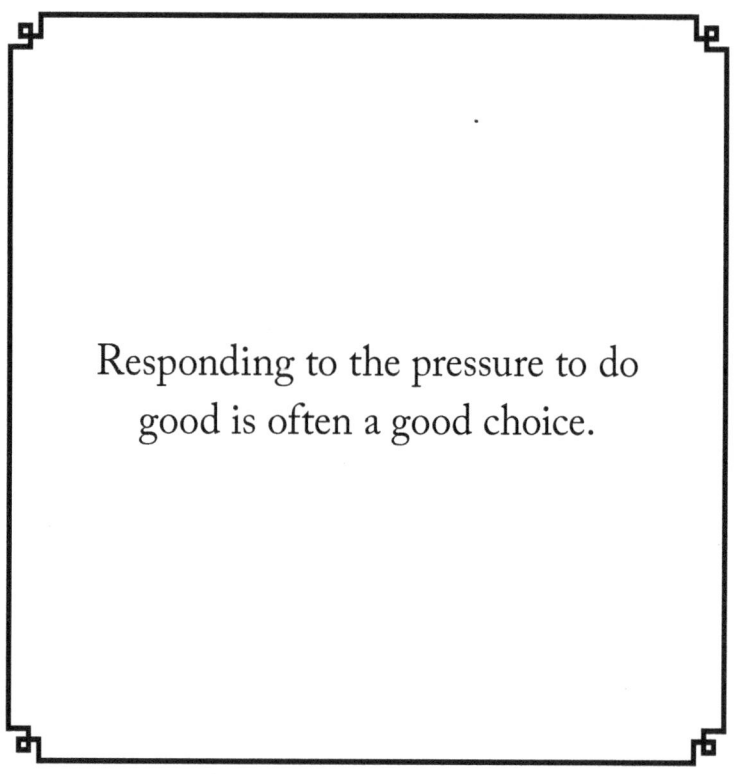

Responding to the pressure to do good is often a good choice.

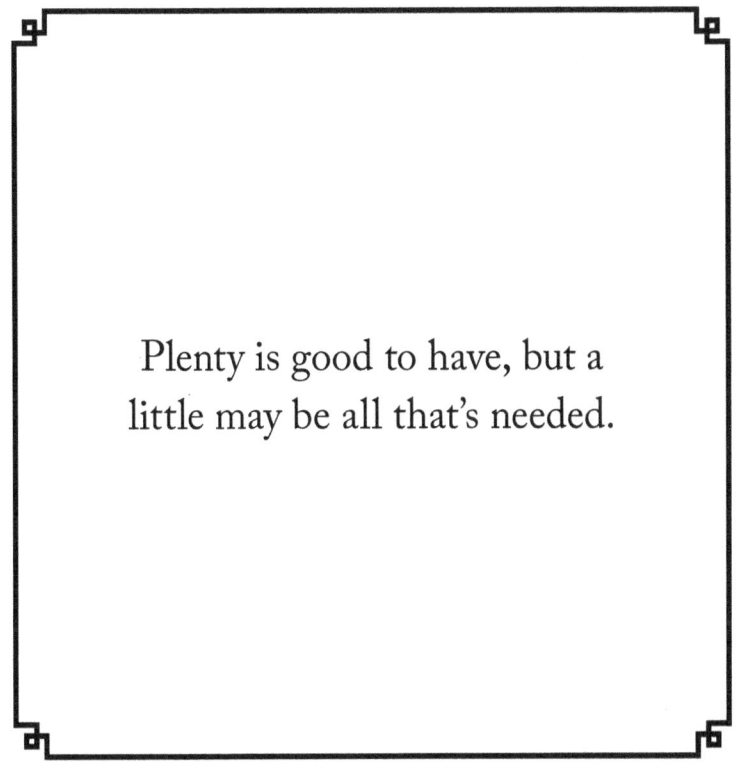

Plenty is good to have, but a little may be all that's needed.

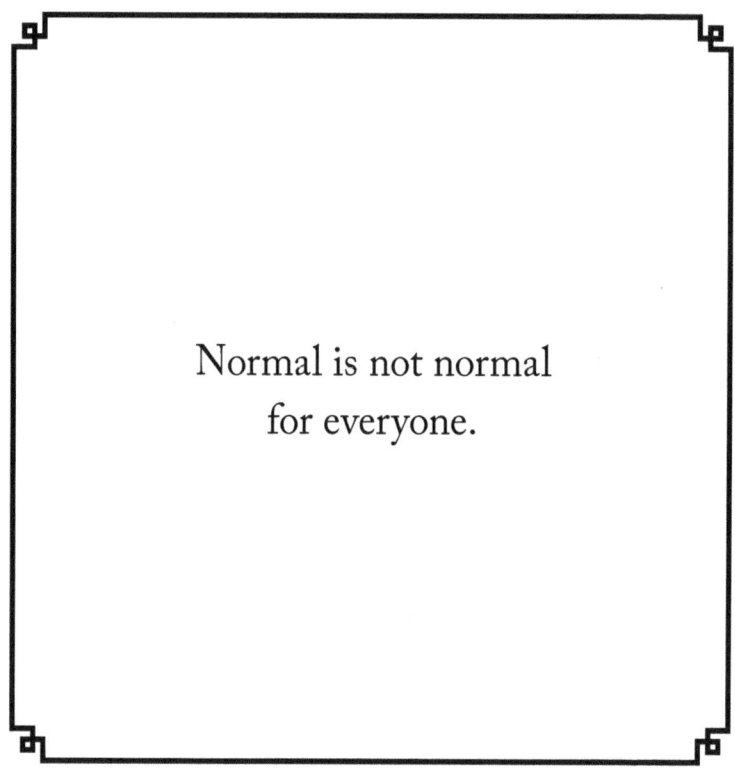

Normal is not normal
for everyone.

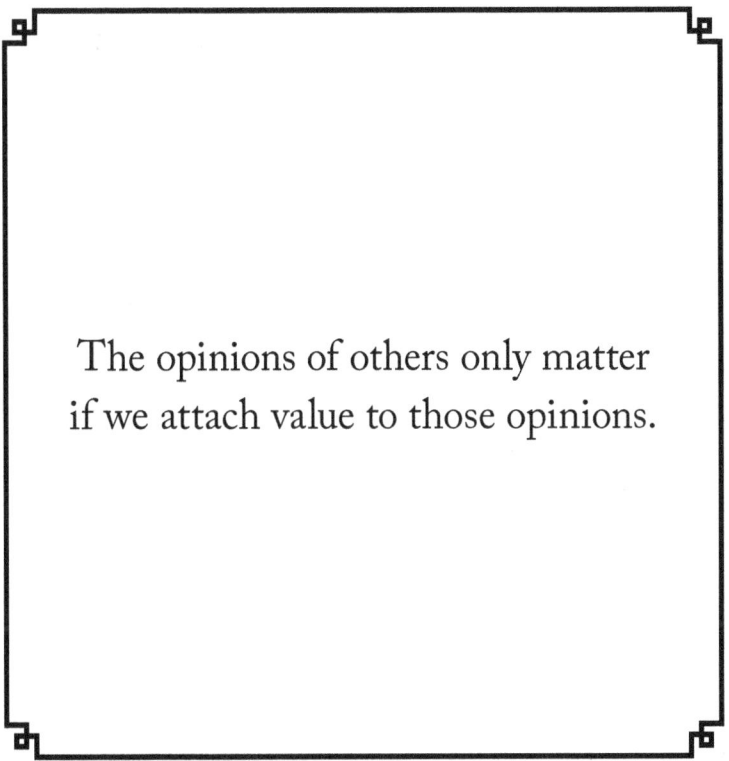

The opinions of others only matter
if we attach value to those opinions.

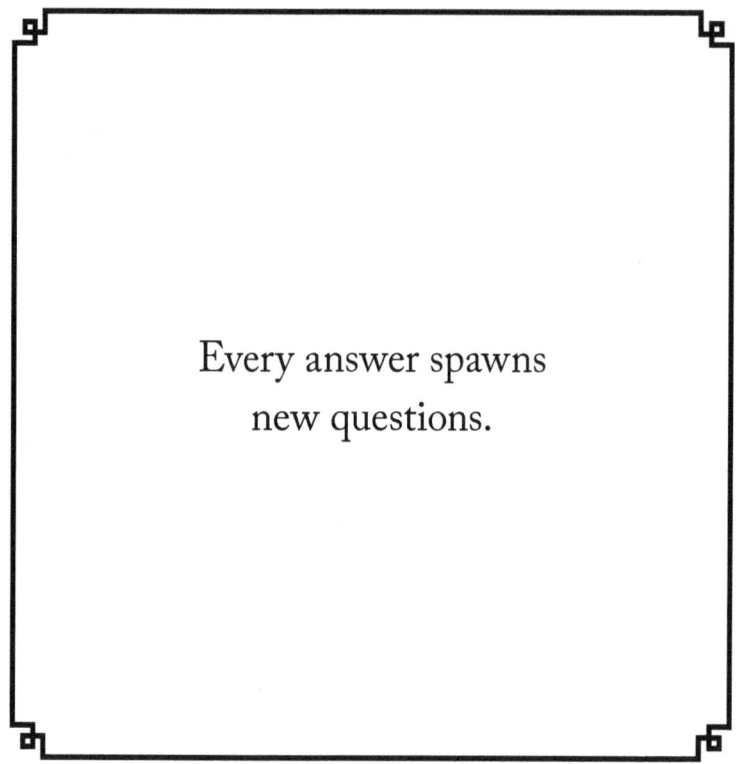

Every answer spawns
new questions.

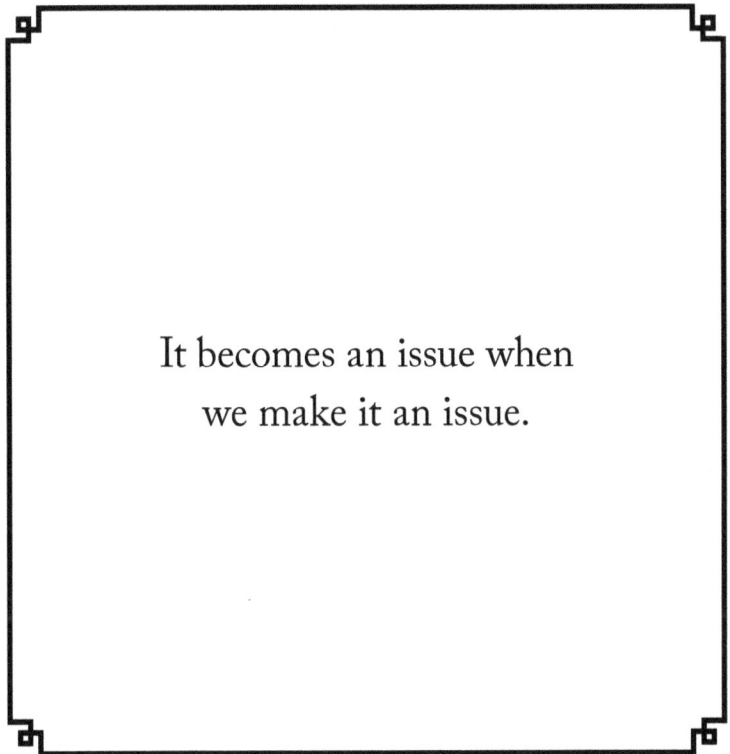

It becomes an issue when
we make it an issue.

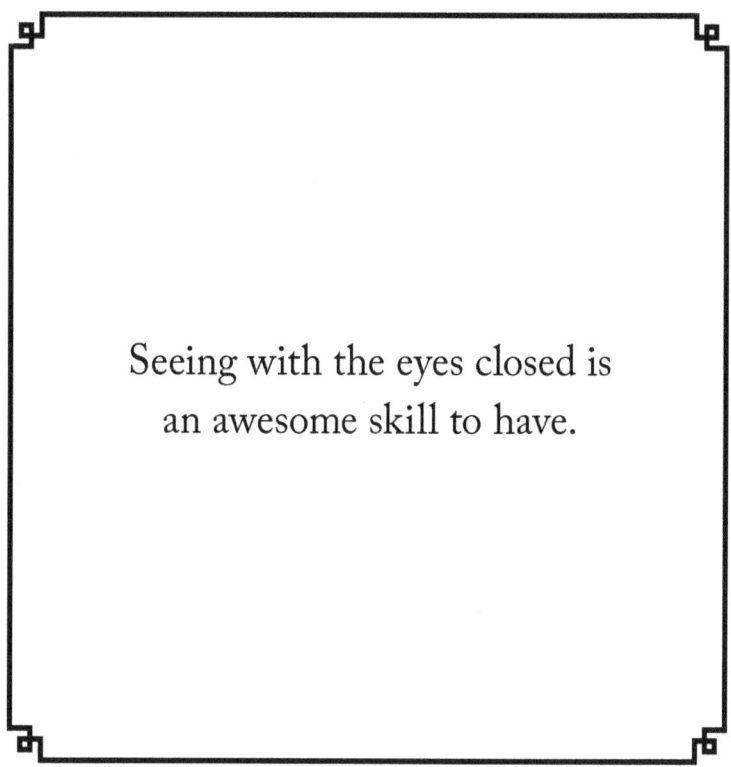

Seeing with the eyes closed is
an awesome skill to have.

Good experiences relived add life to your life. Bad experiences relived could feel like a death blow.

If you look away you might miss important parts of the view... stay focused.

Wild thoughts do not necessarily have to be tamed.... they are like brainstorming for life.

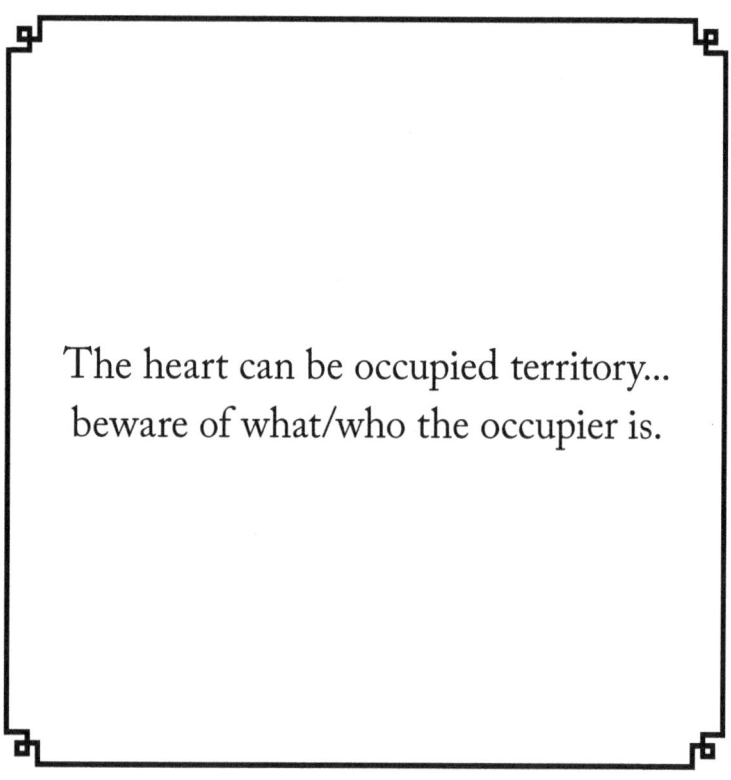

The heart can be occupied territory...
beware of what/who the occupier is.

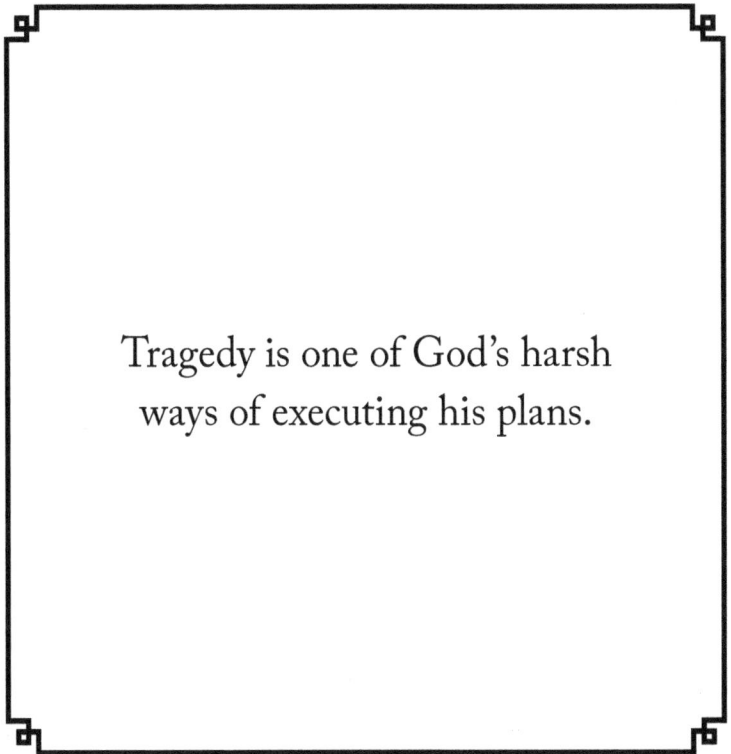

Tragedy is one of God's harsh
ways of executing his plans.

For maintenance of mental sobriety... one should find a quiet spot and have an honest conversation with himself.

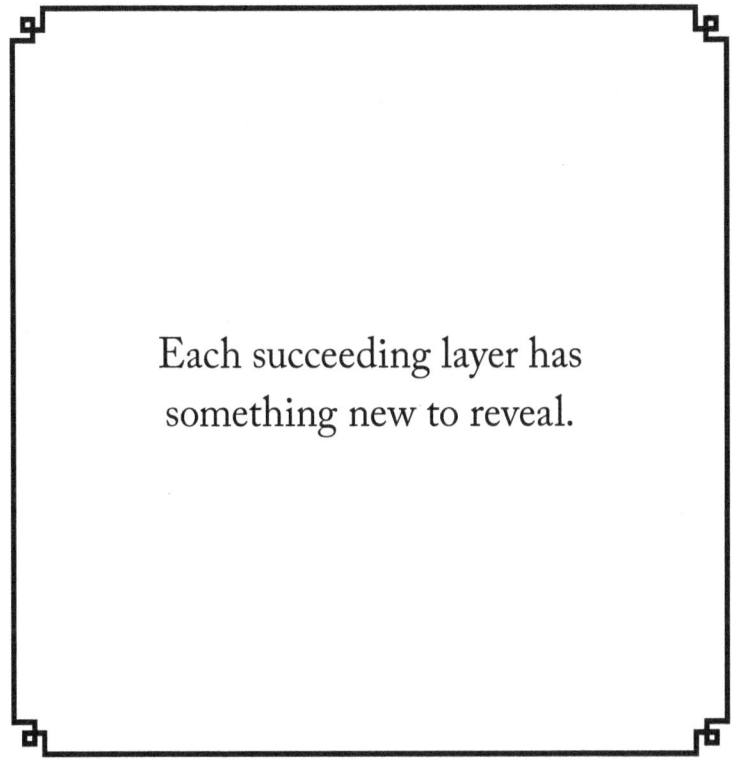

Each succeeding layer has
something new to reveal.

Ends and beginnings have a common meeting point.

Praise a thing only if
it's praiseworthy...

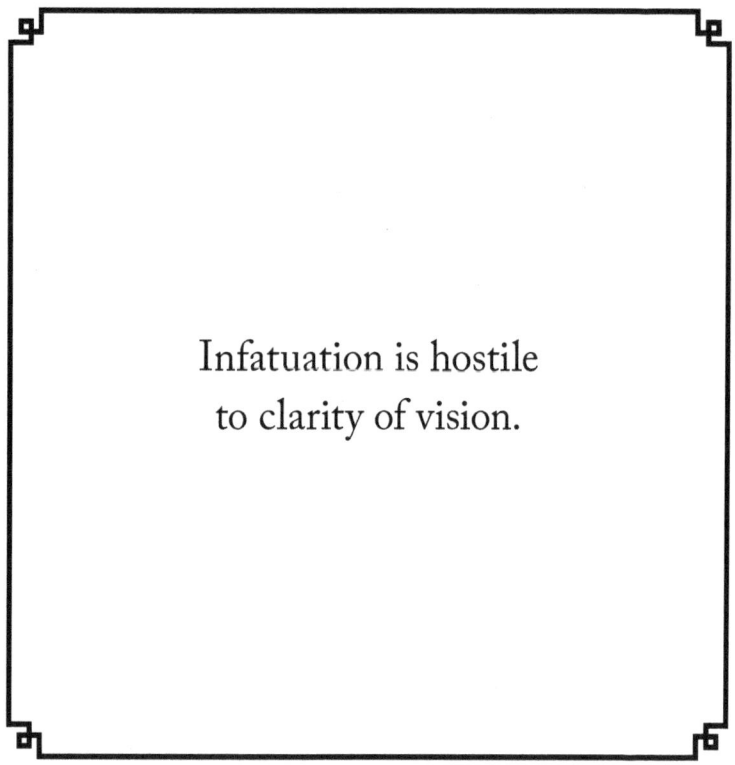

Infatuation is hostile
to clarity of vision.

Sitting sometimes
requires strength.

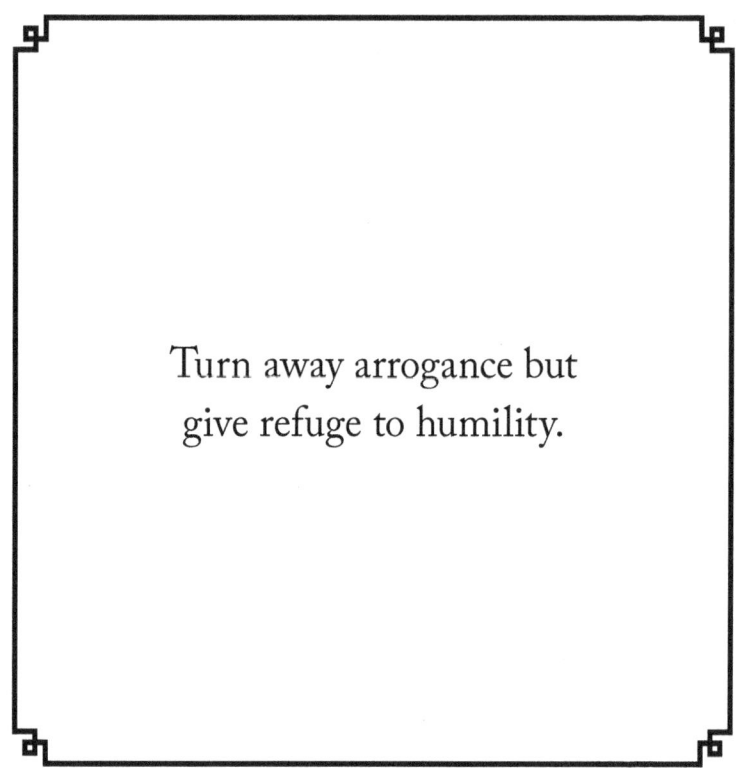

Turn away arrogance but
give refuge to humility.

Should The Conclusion Be That You Are Lost?

.

This is an invitation for you to think along with me. Consider the following scenario: There are a number of ideas floating around in your head. Having ideas in your head is not a new phenomenon. You have had a multiplicity of them since you became cognizant of the notion that ideas do, in fact, take up residence in people's heads. But this time is different. The current ideas in your head are becoming more pervasive, invasive and twitchy; to the point where they are demanding some form of action on your part. Not only are they demanding that you act, they are competing with one another for your attention. These ideas have been there for quite a while, and just as you are undergoing a biological ageing process, they too are growing older and restive. In their ideas minds, they are thinking that you should spare them the indignity of ideas atrophy either by utilizing them or donating them to a more focused ideas host. No self-respecting idea wants to end up in an ideas cemetery without the benefit of having lived his best ideas life.

Remember, these brainchildren of yours are counting on you while creating varying degrees of ruckus to signal their need to be usefully engaged. You are the theatre of this mental plot, and all of this is happening against the backdrop of the other vagaries of your life. Can you relate? You probably can! You may have been on this path before with procrastination as your traveling partner. Remember! An idea is just an idea if it is not brought to life, and not knowing what to do with an idea is just as suffocating to the host as it is to the soul of the idea that hungers to be executed.

The light that's born to the universe exposes things that would otherwise remain unseen and even earns the admiration of objects inanimate in their nature.

"The light that's born to the universe exposes things that would otherwise remain unseen and even earns the admiration of objects inanimate in their nature." - S. Barrock

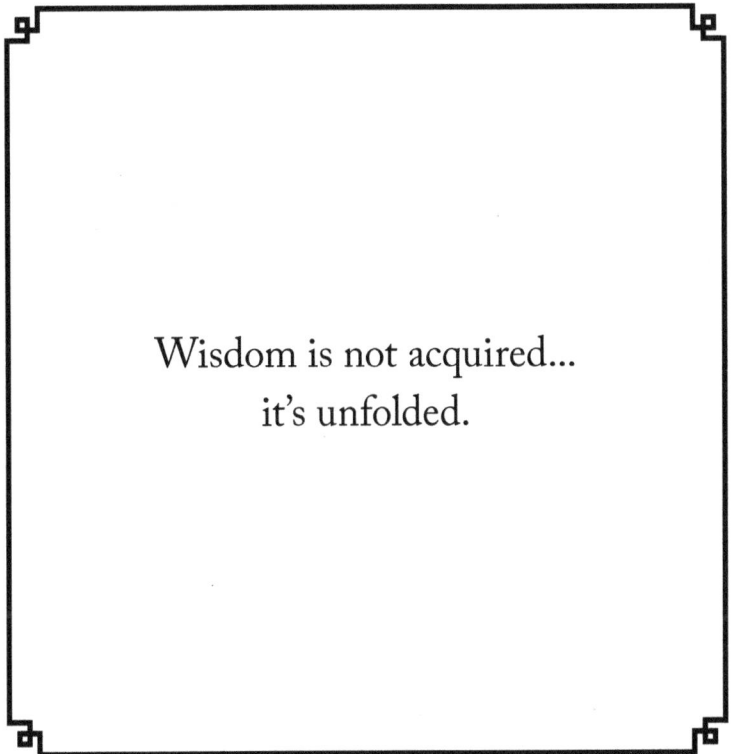

Wisdom is not acquired...
it's unfolded.

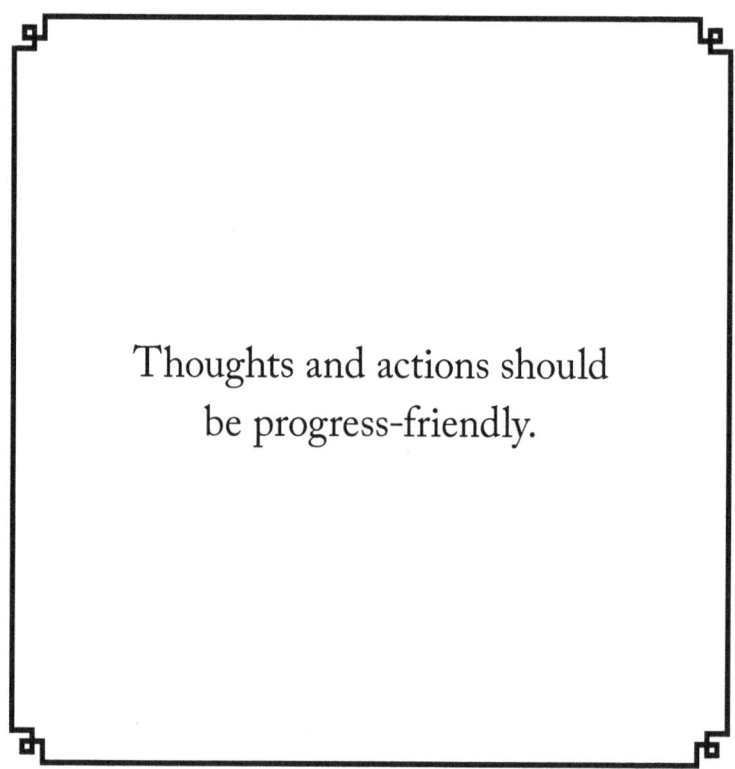

Thoughts and actions should
be progress-friendly.

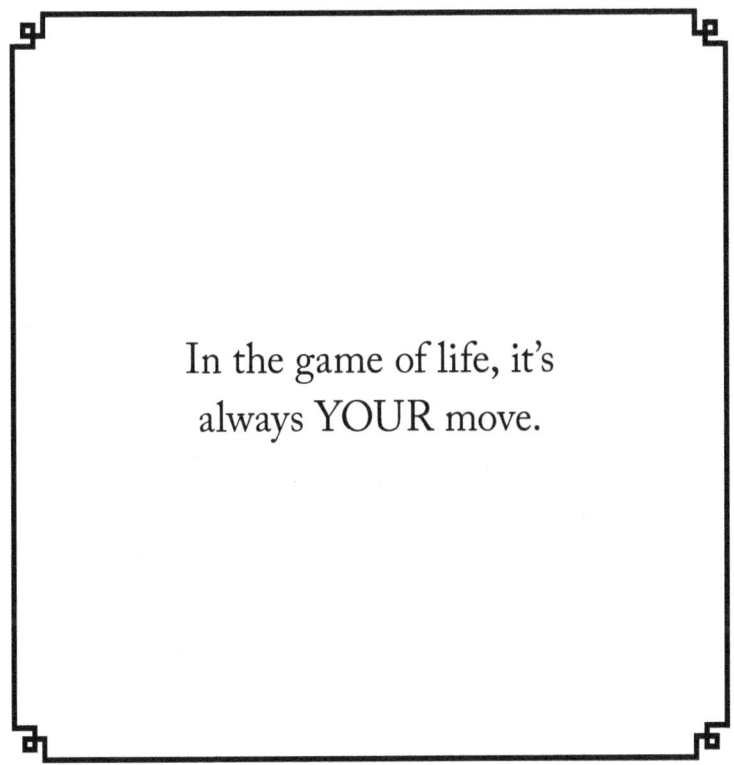

In the game of life, it's
always YOUR move.

Don't do it out of obligation...
do it out of inspiration.

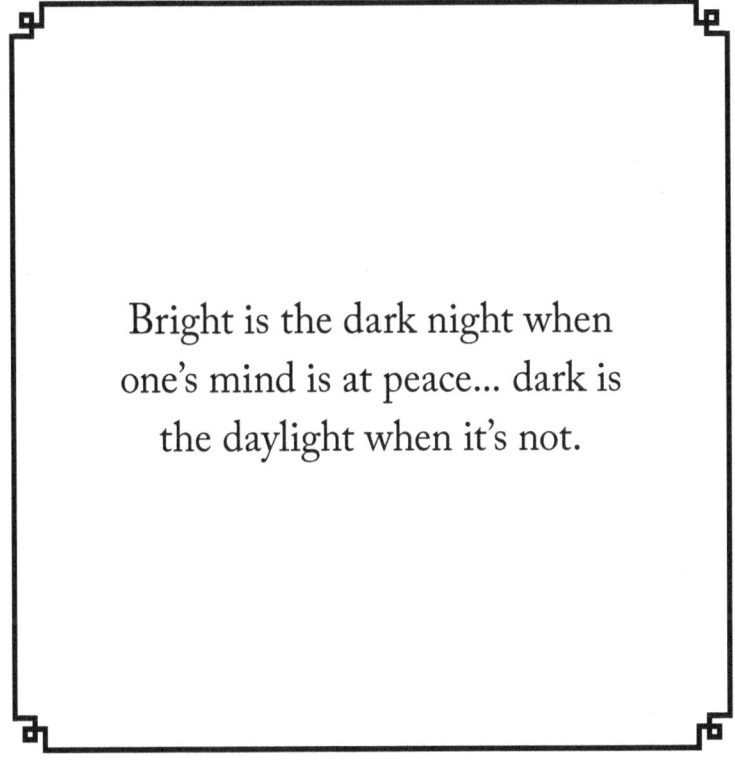

Bright is the dark night when one's mind is at peace... dark is the daylight when it's not.

It's okay for shiny objects to evoke curiosity in the passerby, but closer inspection can reveal how valueless those objects could really be. The true worth of a thing quite often has nothing to do with whether that thing has a shine or not.

Keep all tools handy... there's
much work yet to be done.

We are sustained by the nourishment that passes through the cosmic umbilical cord.

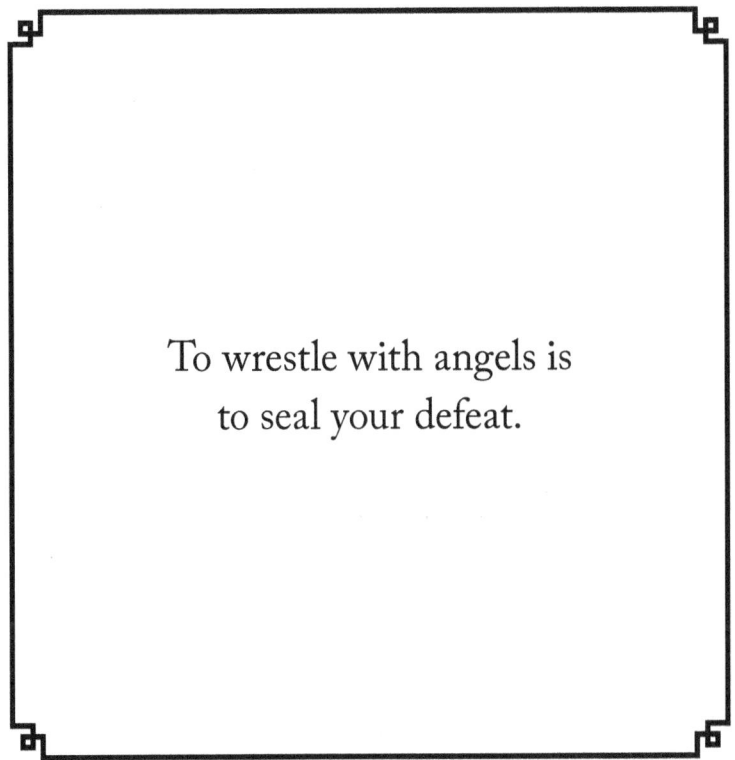

To wrestle with angels is
to seal your defeat.

While doing hard time in the prisons of your minds, your spiritual deaths may occur any time; the deaths of conscience, minds, souls, doing death without parole.

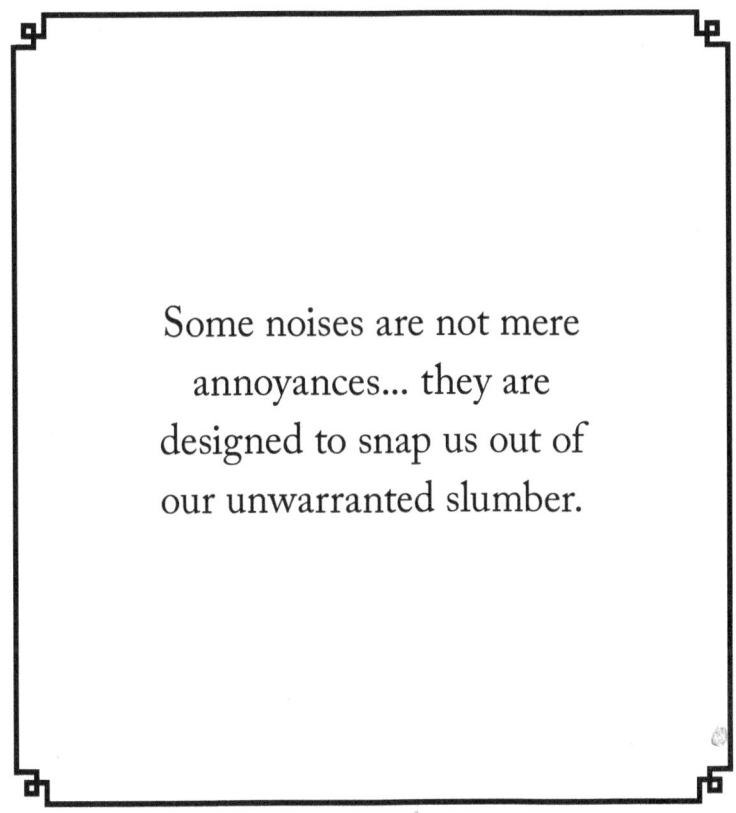

Some noises are not mere annoyances... they are designed to snap us out of our unwarranted slumber.

God in his wisdom has sentenced
us all to life... to live life... but
some through their actions
have chosen to live death.

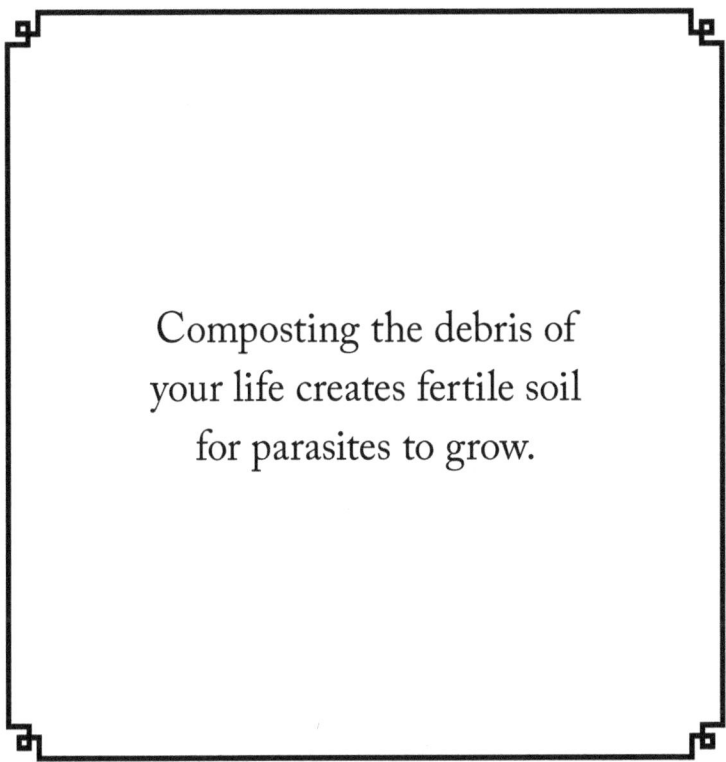

Composting the debris of
your life creates fertile soil
for parasites to grow.

The indistinguishable is a syndrome of symptoms that are individually distinguishable from each other... look deeper to explore each component part.

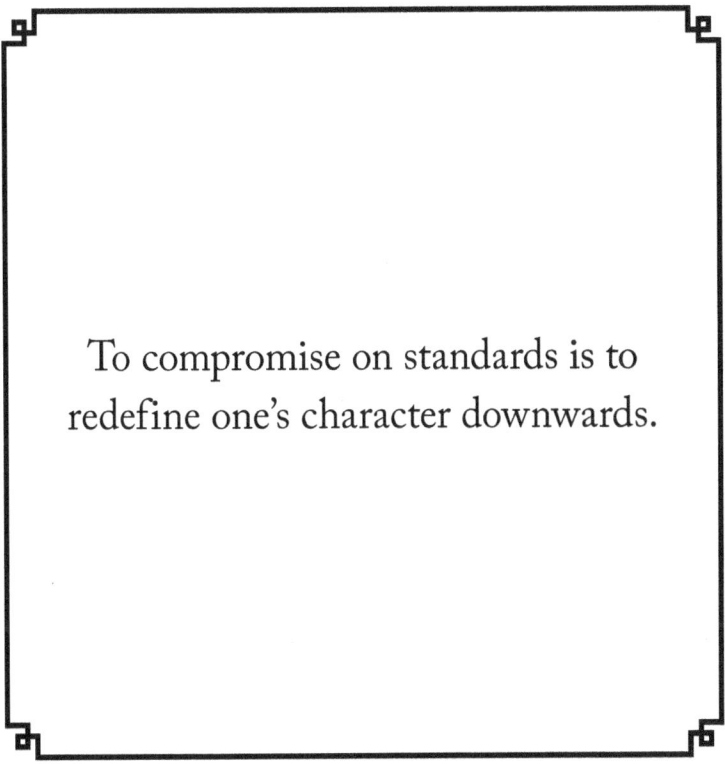

To compromise on standards is to redefine one's character downwards.

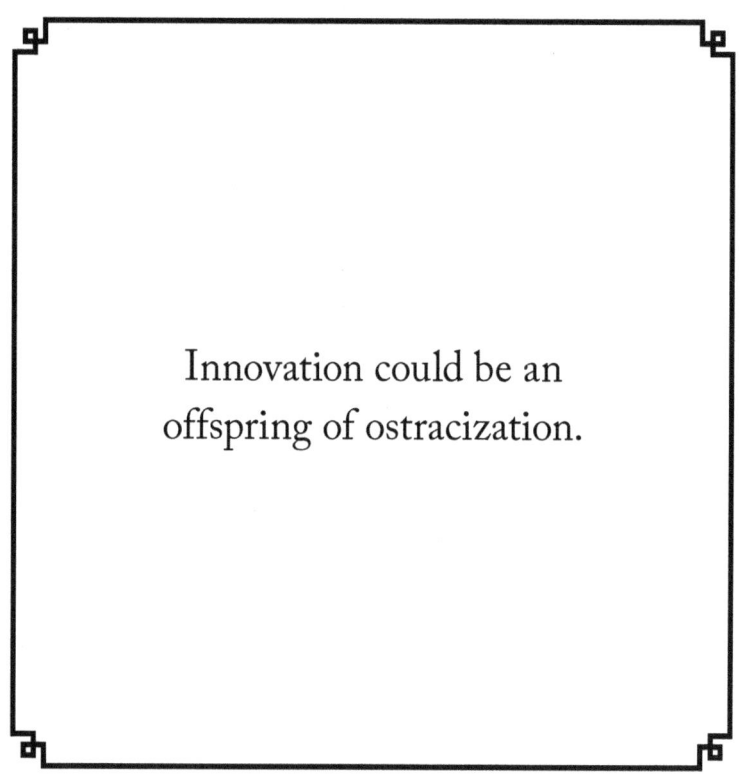

Innovation could be an
offspring of ostracization.

If it comes to the point where one feels as if he is marooned on an uninhabited island, one of his options is to lay claim to the island and have dominion over it.

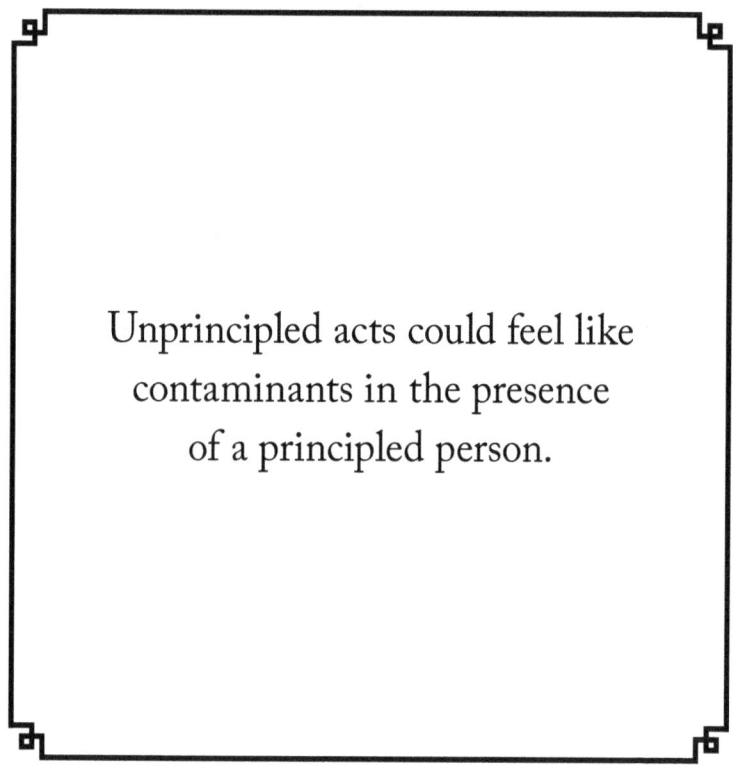

Unprincipled acts could feel like
contaminants in the presence
of a principled person.

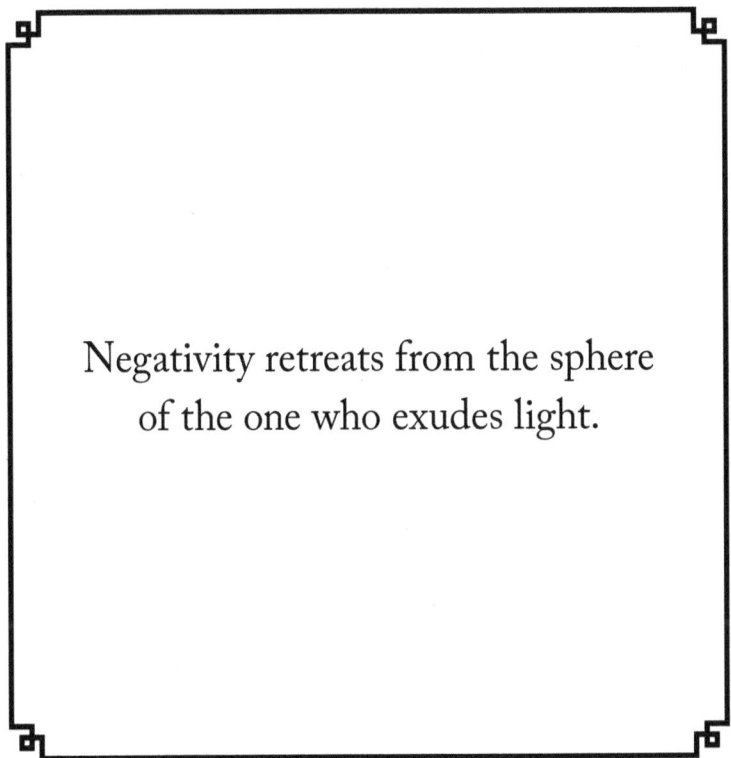

Negativity retreats from the sphere
of the one who exudes light.

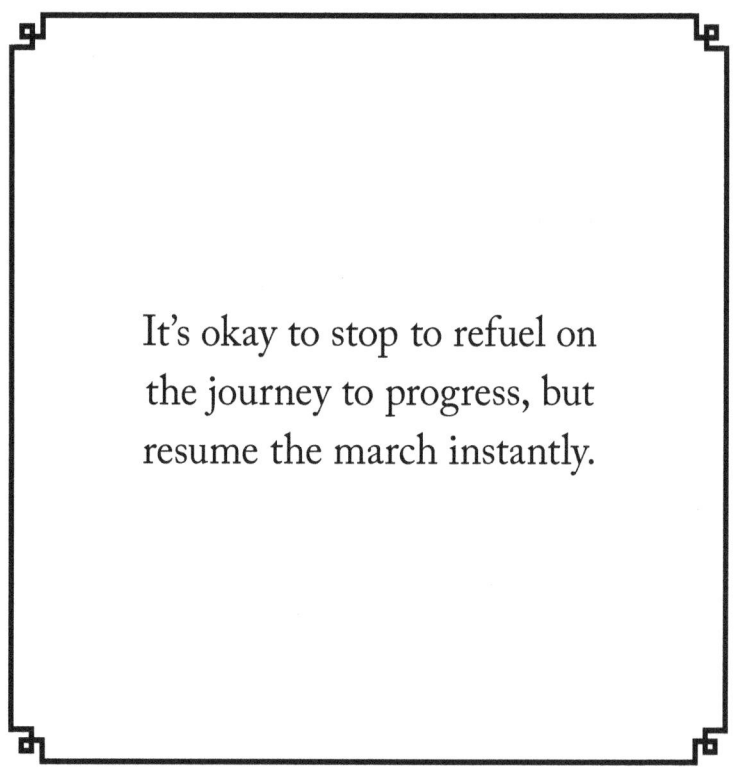

It's okay to stop to refuel on the journey to progress, but resume the march instantly.

People sometimes insist on searching
for things that are not lost.

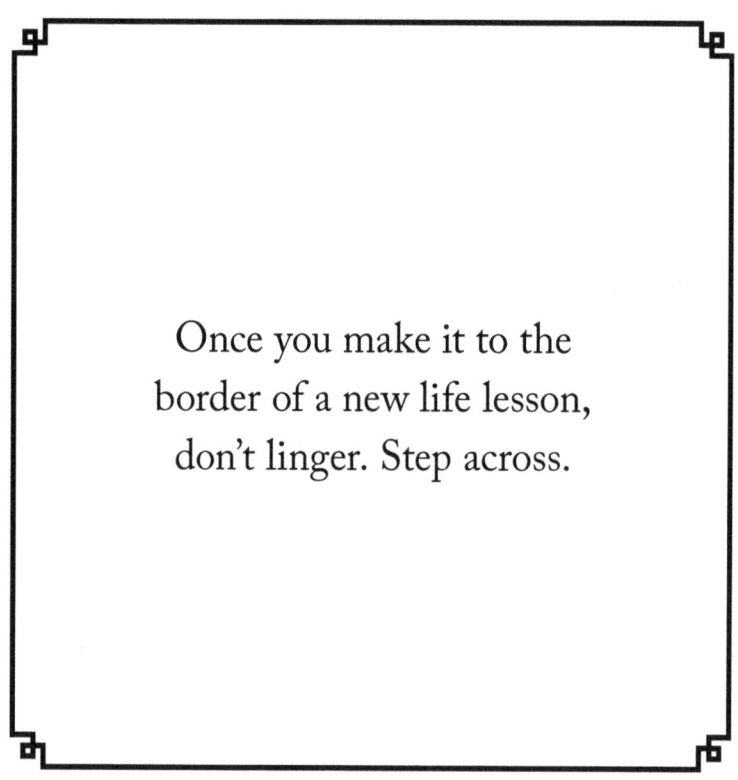

Once you make it to the border of a new life lesson, don't linger. Step across.

One should be a spendthrift when it comes to emotional expenditure for too often that expense falls under the heading of discretionary spending.

Either one finds the missing piece or it will find him... it simply cannot remain missing forever.

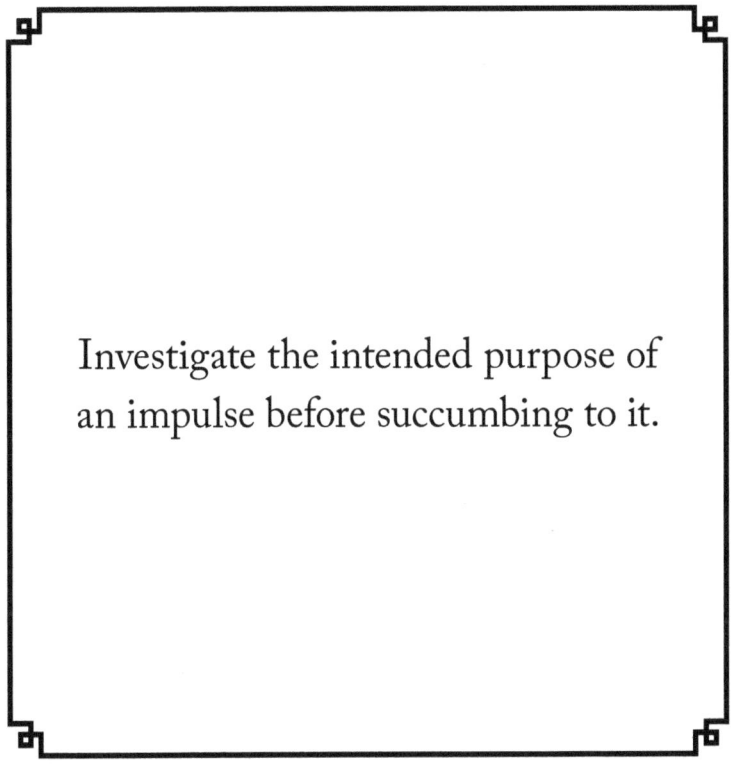

Investigate the intended purpose of an impulse before succumbing to it.

Staircases go up and down and if one finds himself in the middle of the stairs dizzied and confused by the whirling motion of his circumstances, he should pause and compose himself before taking the next step.

Having a hammer doesn't
make one a builder.

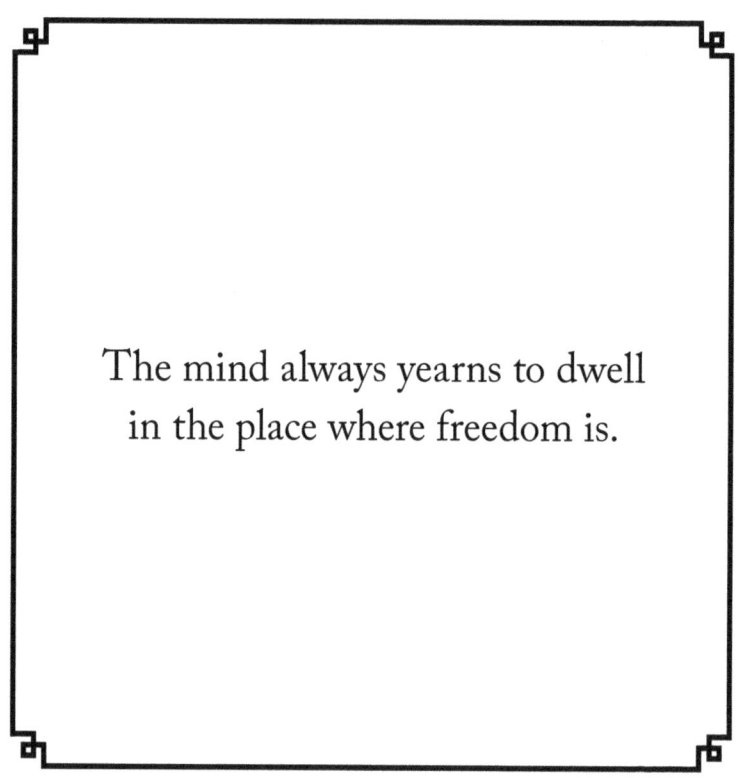

The mind always yearns to dwell
in the place where freedom is.

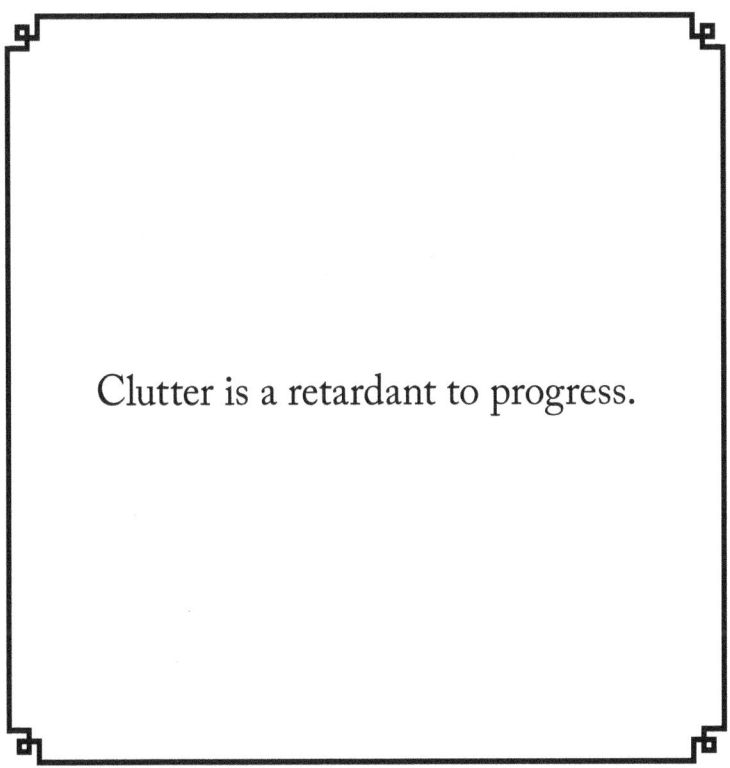

Clutter is a retardant to progress.

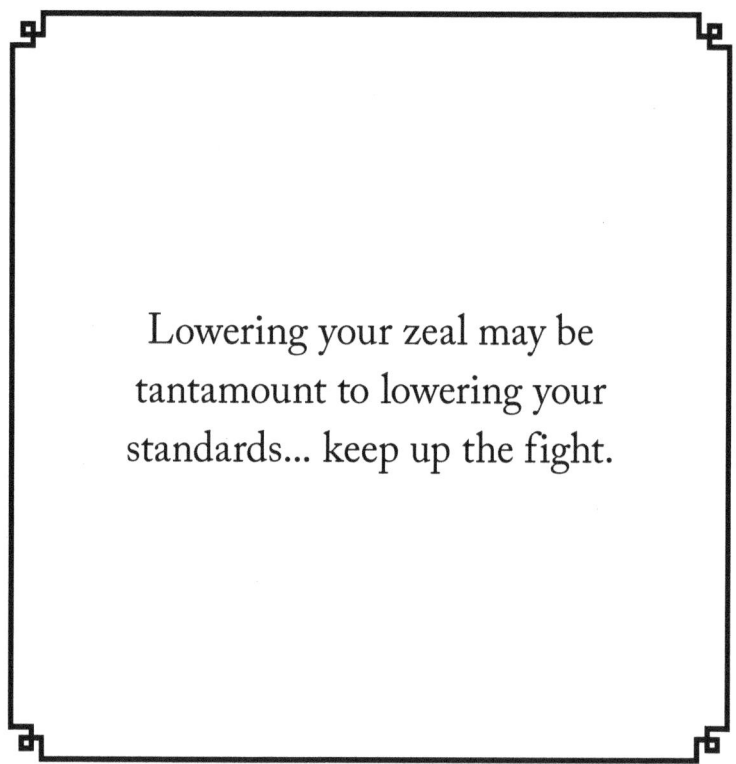

Lowering your zeal may be tantamount to lowering your standards... keep up the fight.

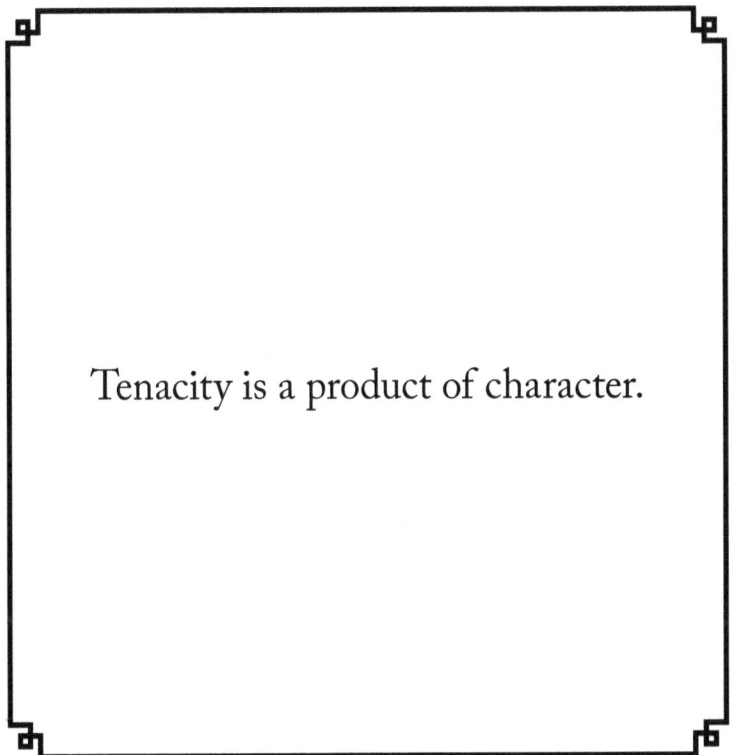

Tenacity is a product of character.

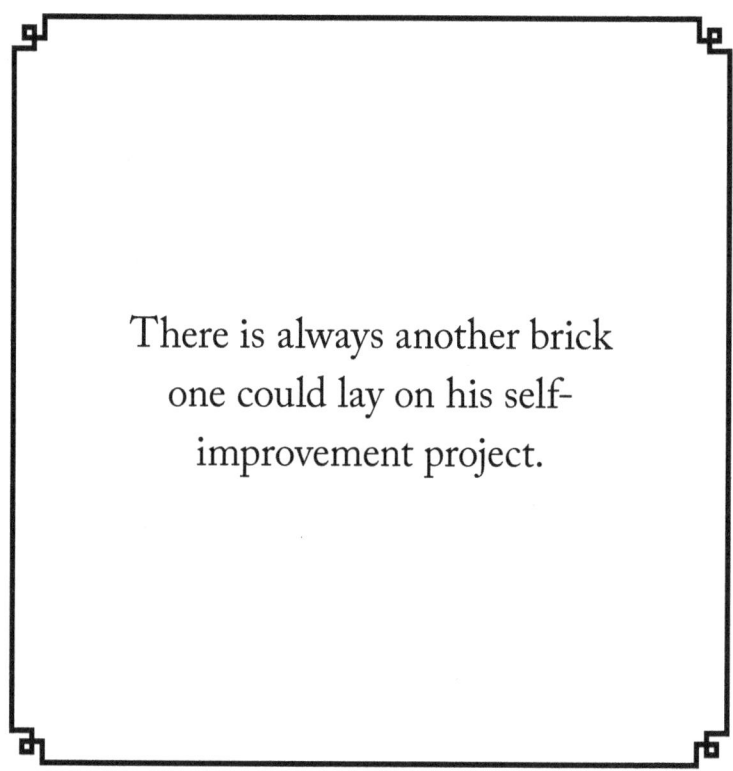

There is always another brick one could lay on his self-improvement project.

If drama somehow makes it to
your guest list, disinvite it.

Just care about somebody...
it's not complicated.

There is always room for
one more blessing.

Bound To Be Free

Bondage can come in different forms. One may find himself in bondage as a result of victimization perpetrated upon him or her by a more powerful force or entity. One could also willingly or unwilling find himself bound by a habit or compunction; in essence volunteering to be bound. Culture or tradition could also be a factor in keeping a person in bondage. Quite apart from cases involving non-mainstream-practices of living out fetishes and fantasies through bondage, it would be reasonable to say that every bound person has an innate desire to be free. Bondage imposes strictures, stagnation and retardation, and is openly aggressive toward upward mobility. Presuming we endorse the view that freedom is the opposite of bondage, then to be unbound is to be free – free to dream, to walk, to talk, and to come to the realization that you are a valued traveler in the realm of an infinite universe. It is in this unbound state that one could recognize and work towards breaking the spell of bondage. Yes, bondage is representative of a spell, a curse, and in the absence of awareness, a designation of lifelong self-limitation. Some people reading this might be able to classify themselves as being either bound or free or somewhere in between. If you are in between, it could make a difference whether your current position reflects a movement from bondage to freedom or from freedom to bondage. You have to decide which direction you are moving towards in order to clarify the actions you need to take to either prevent further decent or keep on the trajectory upwards to freedom. Freedom has its own set of qualifiers, as well, for a person could be physically free while being mentally bound, and vice versa. It is said that mental bondage is worse than physical bondage because an imprisoned mind is one devoid of dynamism and suitable functionality. It is understandable when some people are justly imprisoned as punishment for breaking societal norms and rules. Most of these people will, once again, see the light of day upon completing their sentences and reclaim their freedoms to pursue whatever enterprise interests them. The institution of Human Slavery - unbelievable bondage - and its progenies are so antithetical to anything that is humanly perceptible, that God himself must often struggle with having to admit that he had anything to do with the creation of the brains that developed the concepts of inflicting such torture on fellow humans. Human Slavery is second to none in its degeneracy, so I will not deal with it here. When one is born into a culture or family that has not been psychologically cleared to imagine high achievement because of a tradition of restricted vision for success, that person may automatically subscribe to this self-limiting ideal. His forebears didn't engage their freedom to imagine greatness, so he followed the same path. This is a kind of self-bondage that can be fixed with a new awareness and the development of a zeal and zest for a fuller life. Once one member of the group or family discovers and demonstrates the possibilities that a free mind can engender, he becomes a pioneer for the others to travel that same pathway, thereby breaking that generational curse. Even though success may look different for everyone in a material sense, the freedom to follow the path to that success is a success in itself. Bondage has a finite lifespan because it's often a negative imposed on an individual, but freedom is infinite because it is one with the Cosmos.

"It is at the point of confident anticipation where obscurity gradually gives way to clarity." - S. Barrock

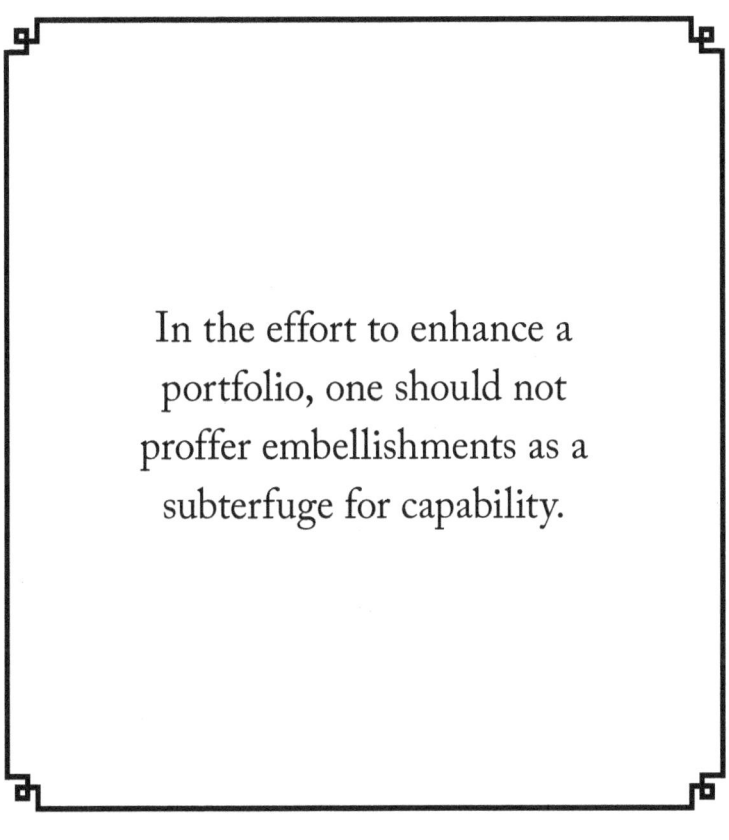

In the effort to enhance a portfolio, one should not proffer embellishments as a subterfuge for capability.

The mental space one provides
for new content should be
free of unwanted material.

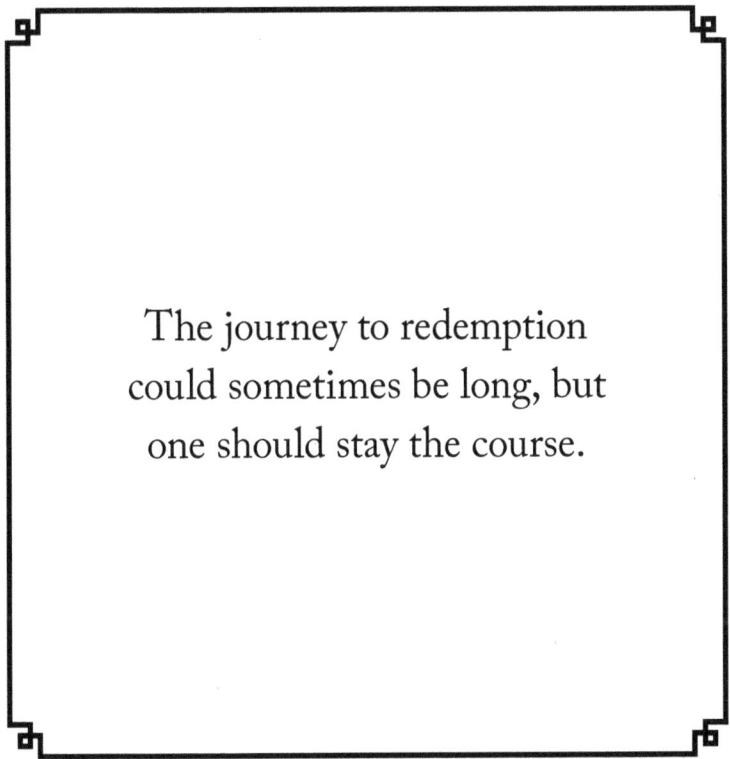

The journey to redemption could sometimes be long, but one should stay the course.

It's not ethical to claim to possess exceptional eyesight when the day itself is unusually clear.

Forces propel us in the direction
of our thoughts. The nature
of our thoughts is in direct
correlation to the force.

An unrepentant soul is guaranteed to live a tormented life even if it doesn't always show on the outside.

Your body... your mind... your spirit
are all part of your own unique
constituency. Make sure you listen
to what they are telling you.

Check your mental inbox daily and delete unwanted material. Check your mental spam folder as well... it is funny how useful material could be hidden among worthless ones.

An aura of goodness surrounds you... do not miss any opportunity to frolic in it.

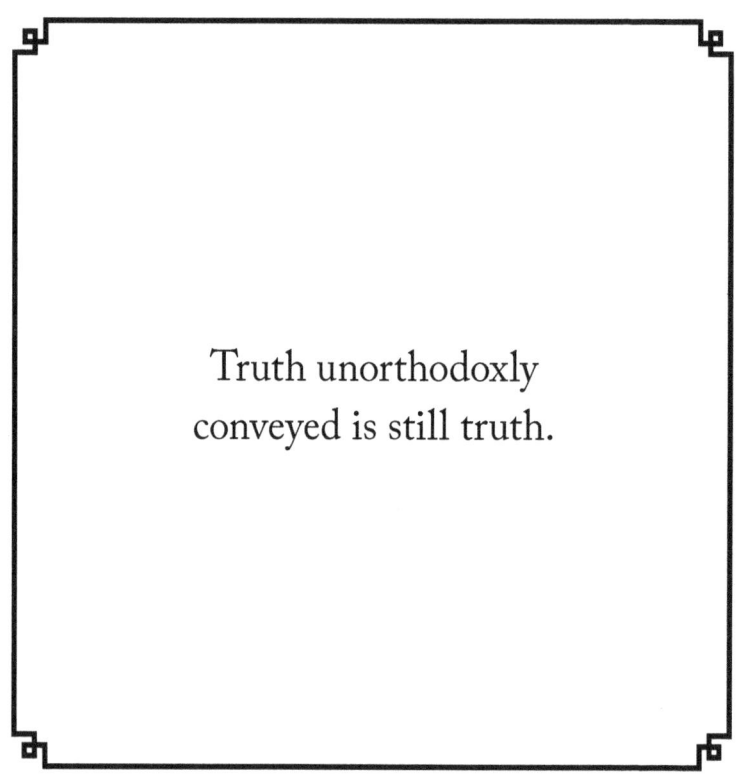

Truth unorthodoxly
conveyed is still truth.

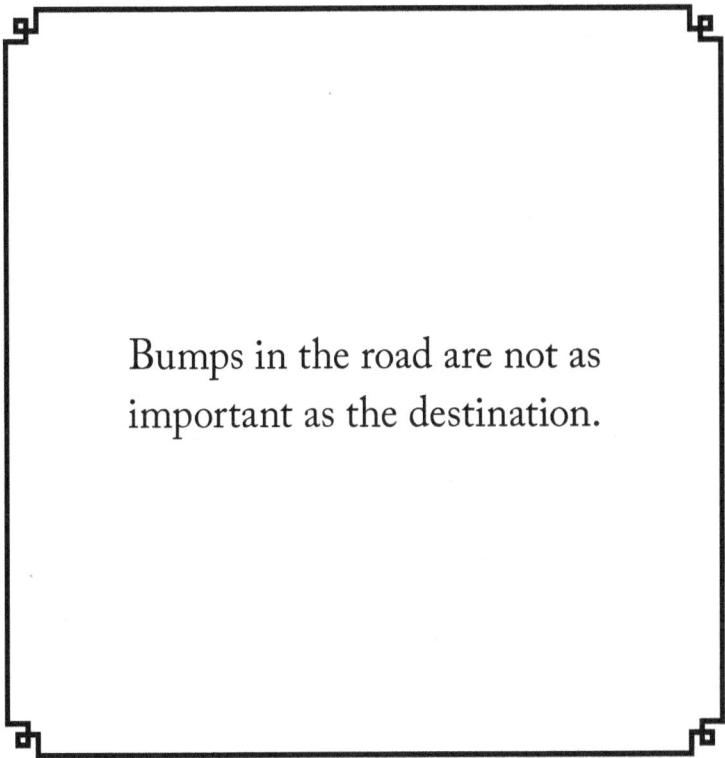

Bumps in the road are not as important as the destination.

Good news does not always
arrive in pretty packages.

The simple act of listening to someone's story could be the thing that fills the void in her soul.

One cannot always lead and one cannot always follow, but one can decide how he wants to lead and how he wants to be led.

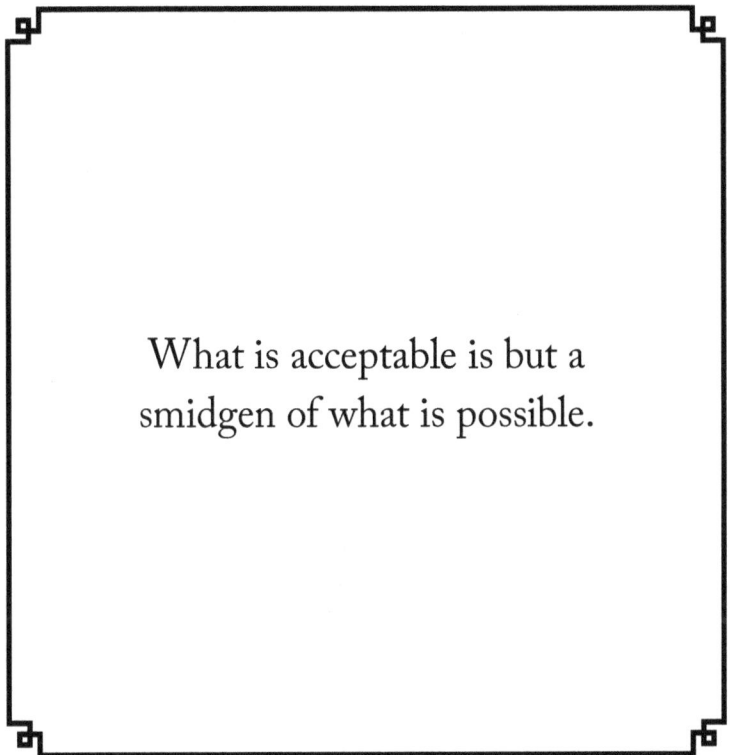

What is acceptable is but a
smidgen of what is possible.

The bar is not very high if winning in a tit-for-tat argument is determined by who gets the last tat.

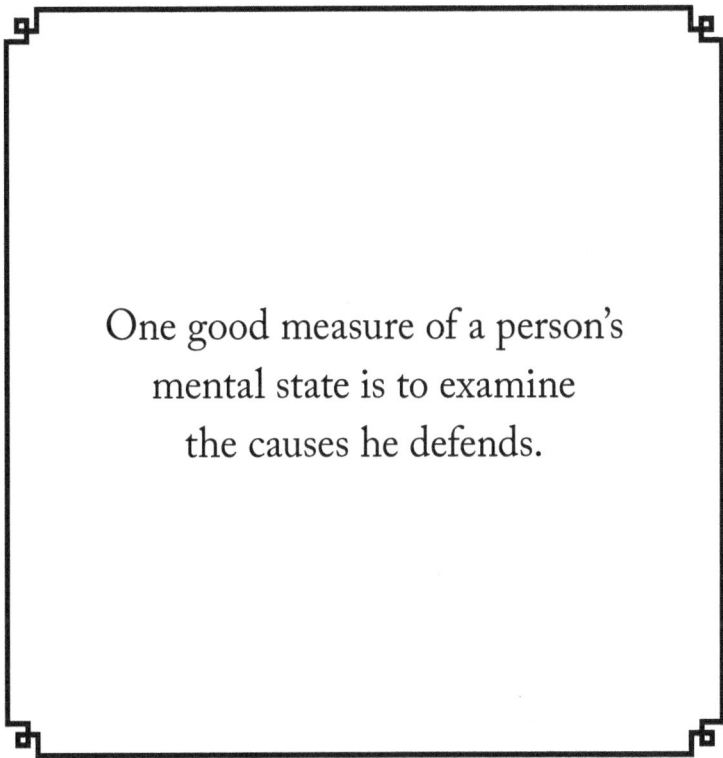

One good measure of a person's
mental state is to examine
the causes he defends.

Every misfortune is not attributable to a misstep... misfortunes test our resolve and help us build character... missteps are unwitting steps in the direction of learning.

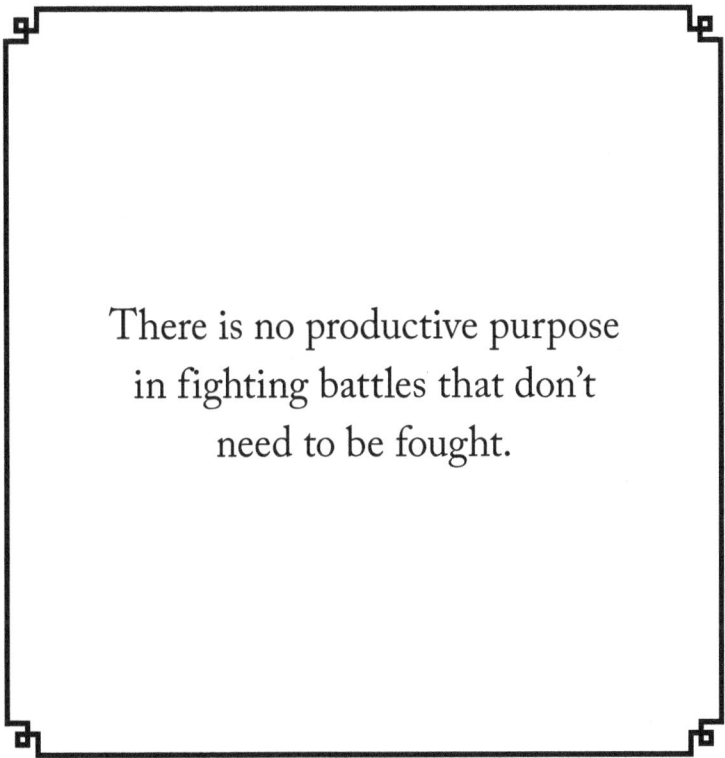

There is no productive purpose in fighting battles that don't need to be fought.

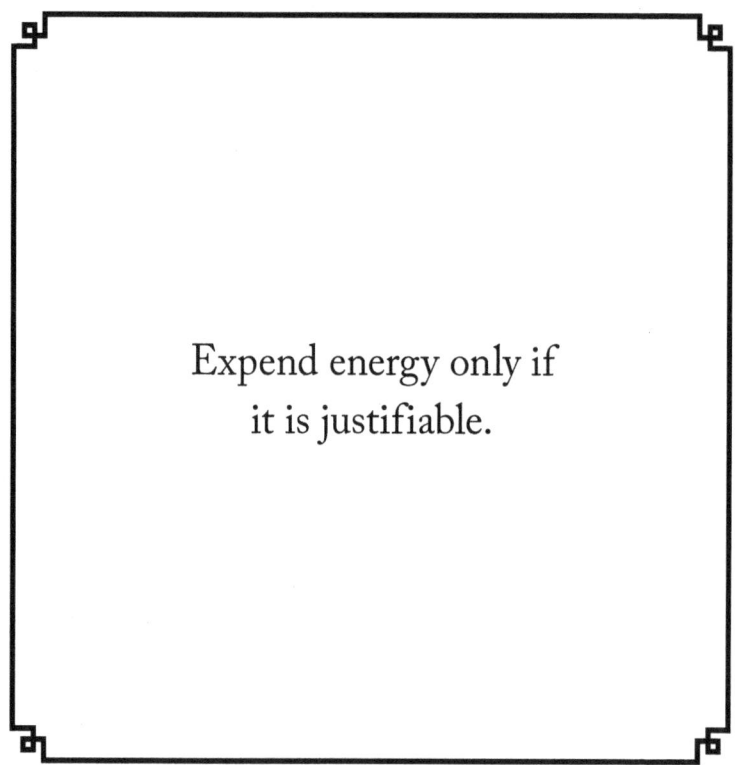

Expend energy only if
it is justifiable.

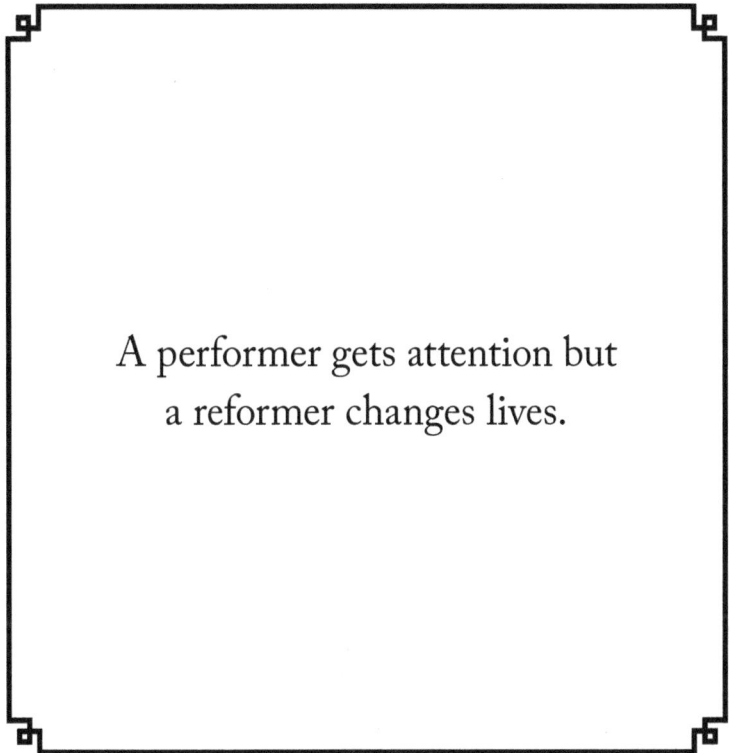

A performer gets attention but
a reformer changes lives.

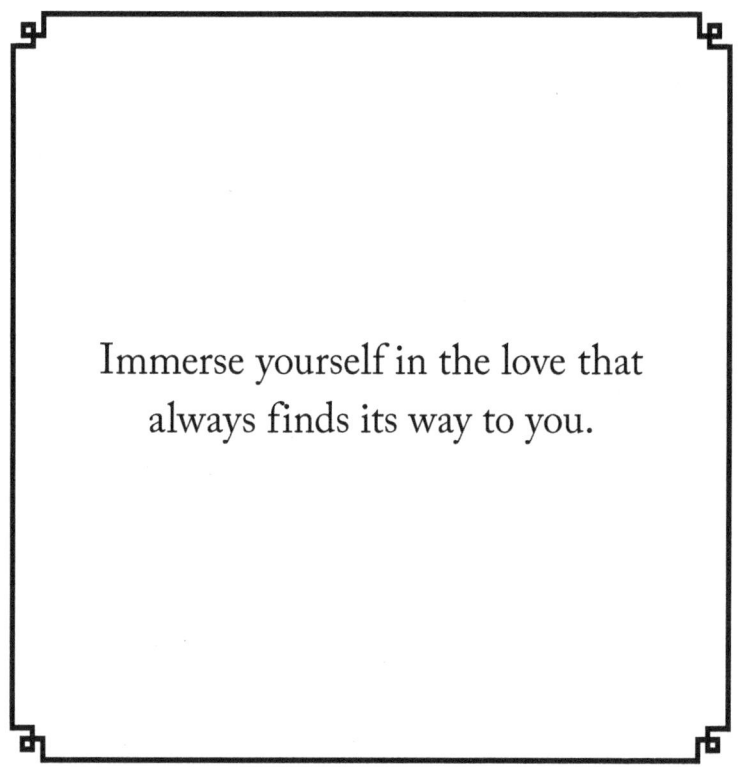

Immerse yourself in the love that always finds its way to you.

Tally - up the challenges you overcame at the end of each day, and you will see that you are more durable than you think you are.

If you look away you might miss some parts of the view... stay focused.

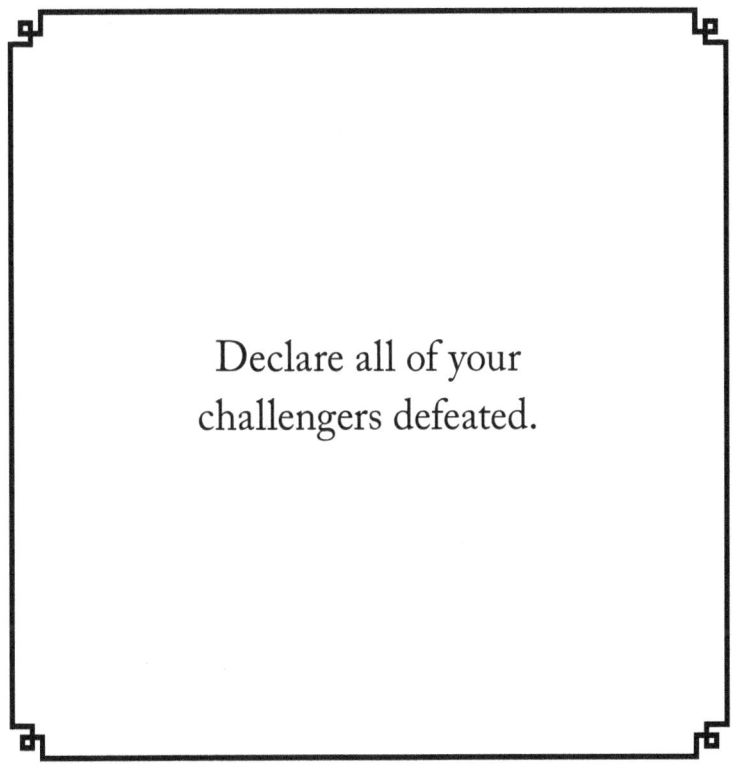

Declare all of your
challengers defeated.

The opinions of others only matter
if we attach value to those opinions.

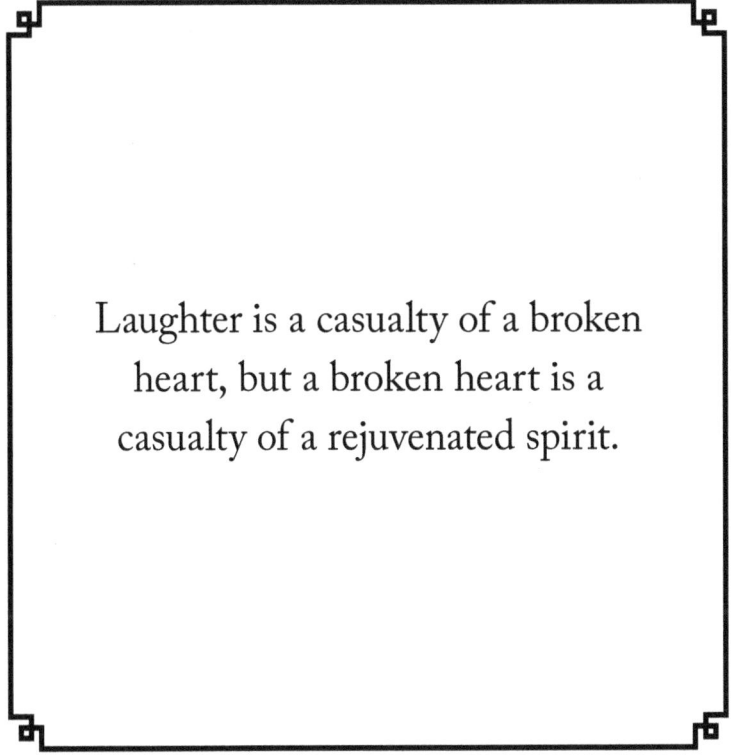

Laughter is a casualty of a broken heart, but a broken heart is a casualty of a rejuvenated spirit.

All of the bricks on a building are not cornerstones, but each row of bricks gives support to the rows above it.

Many people spend an inordinate amount of time trying to distance themselves from their own truths only to experience a head-on encounter with those very truths somewhere down the road.

The one who endeavors to sustain a corruptive environment is a dispenser of bitter potions.

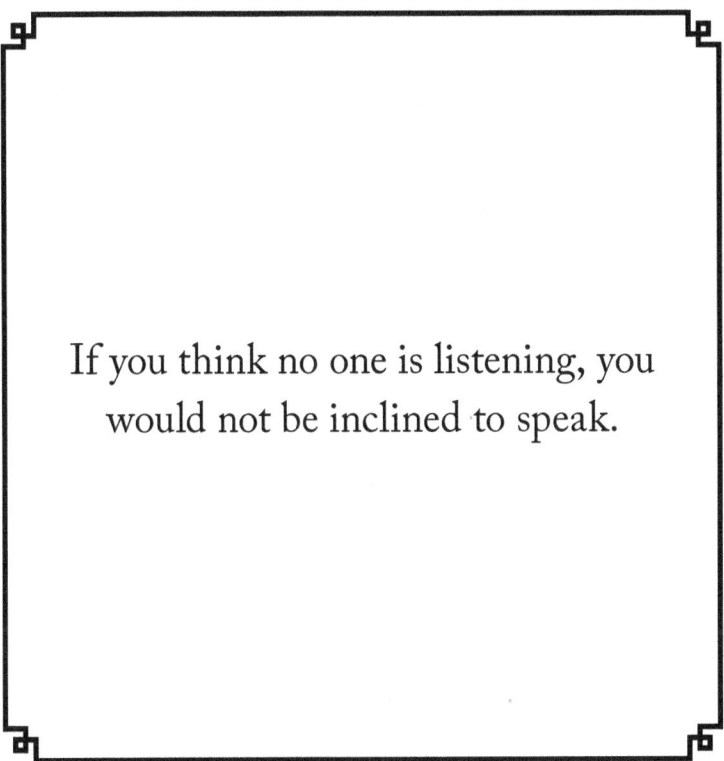

If you think no one is listening, you would not be inclined to speak.

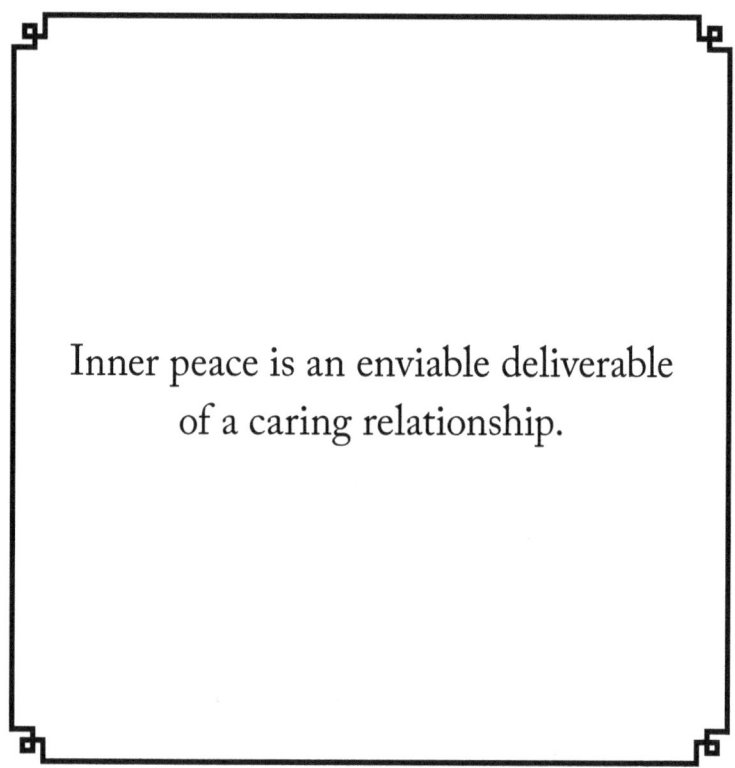

Inner peace is an enviable deliverable of a caring relationship.

To Date Or Not To Date

Lately you have been in a reflective mood. You have had a long-term marriage which lasted for eight years. You first got married at the age of twenty. Your spouse was your high school sweetheart and you two were madly in love with each other. You gave birth to a son at age twenty-two. Six years later tragedy befell your family. Your beloved husband developed a brain aneurism and died the next day. Dealing with that loss was so intense that you even entertained the idea that had it not been for your son, you would find no purpose in continuing to live. Five years went by, and you were able to pull yourself together enough to start working on self- improvement; going to the gym and enrolling in college. Although you did not feel like you were ready for a new romantic relationship, occasional bouts of loneliness would creep up on you. Deflecting and suppressing the urges that would accompany the episodes of loneliness worked up to a point. However, the frequency and intensity of these urges increased. Ultimately, deflecting and suppressing were no longer viable options. You resorted to innovative ways of dealing with these pulls in the absence of a romantic relationship. This practice grew old, too, and you started dating someone you met at the gym. He did not really want a serious relationship, but you became sexually involved with him anyway. In a matter of two months, you found yourself being pregnant again. This time you are pregnant for someone who was never introduced to your family or had ever met your son. Someone who, in fact, had a wife and family that you never knew about! In essence you were having a fling, and this was out of character for you. You started your romantic life in a healthy, loving way. Now you are brought to a point of desperation as a result of another point of desperation. How would you explain this situation to your son and other close relatives? Your good character took an internal hit as it surprised even you that you could allow this to happen. You are now faced with making a moral or a practical choice. A moral choice would satisfy the pious people in your life. They would say have the baby because that's the way God would want it. This is the so-called 'right-to-life' group who considers it sinful to abort a baby. This is the group that says have the baby no matter the circumstances under which it was conceived. The practical choice, according to the so-called 'right-to-choose' group, might be to terminate the pregnancy and give yourself a chance to learn from your mistake and go on with your life. In either case, the psychological fallout is unescapable, so it takes a period of reflecting and planning, and self-forgiveness in order to reach a point of wholeness, People regularly make wrong turns in their lives, and the greatest condemnation one could experience is the one where he chooses to condemn himself. Those who are in the business of condemning others for redeemable faults should honestly look within themselves to discover their own hidden demons. To the pious people among us – many of whom are churchgoers – just remember Jesus admonished you to 'cast the first stone if you are without sin. Life can be complex yet simple. The extent to which we understand how opposite forces can be at play, at the same time, in the same person, is what sharpens our vision to see more clearly how to cope and recognize the meaning in each experience. Weakness is really strength that is under construction, and not every situation or outcome can be planned with one- hundred percent accuracy. The unforeseen will, with time, become the seen, and life will be decidedly drab in the absence of both the seen and the unseen.

"The pathway to higher consciousness is always illuminated, but too often we fear stepping into that clearly visible space and choose instead

to hide in the shadows." - S. Barrock

When a person insists on playing the
role of antagonist in his own story,
his misery is not likely to abate.

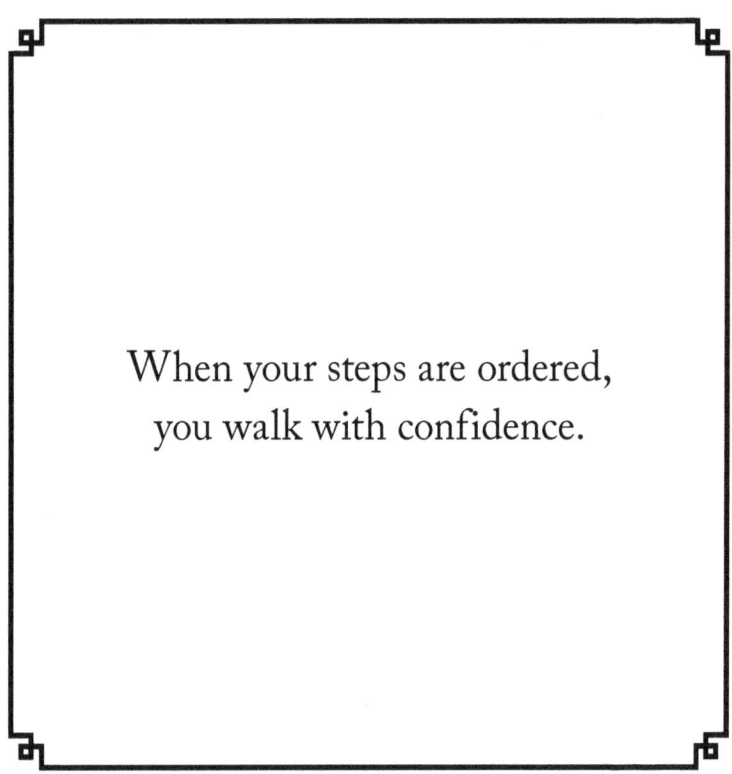

When your steps are ordered,
you walk with confidence.

In every barrier erected a
weakness will be detected.

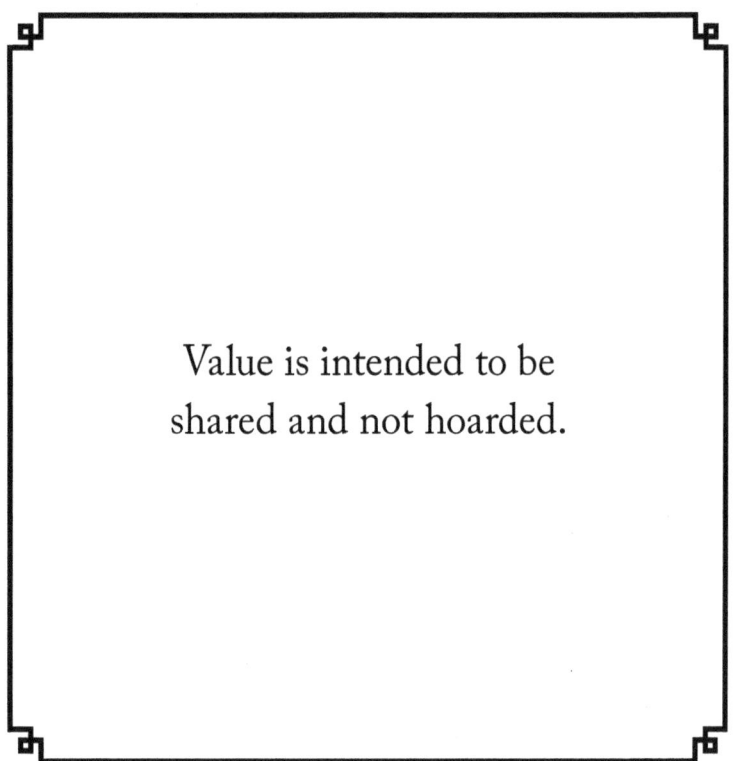

Value is intended to be
shared and not hoarded.

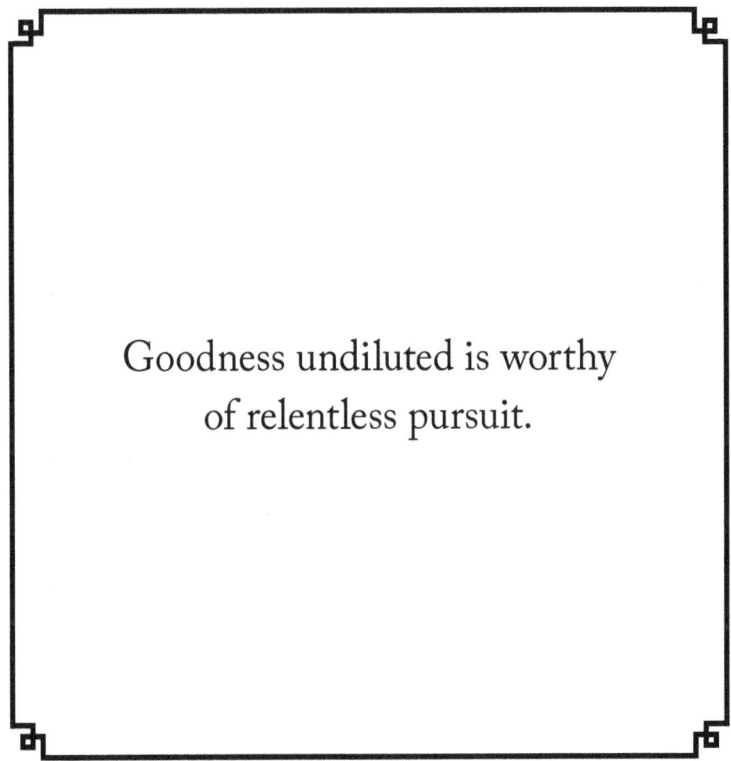

Goodness undiluted is worthy
of relentless pursuit.

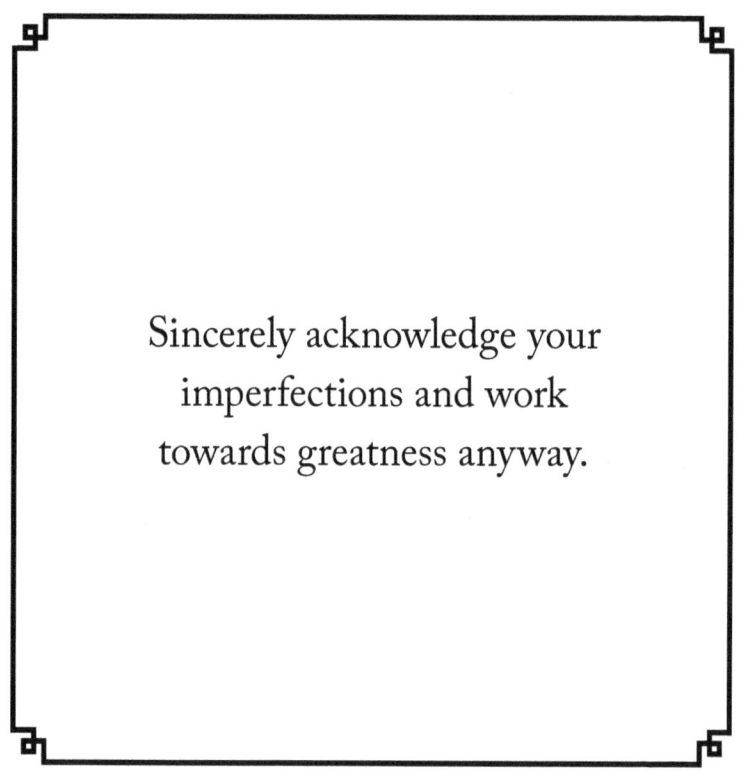

Sincerely acknowledge your imperfections and work towards greatness anyway.

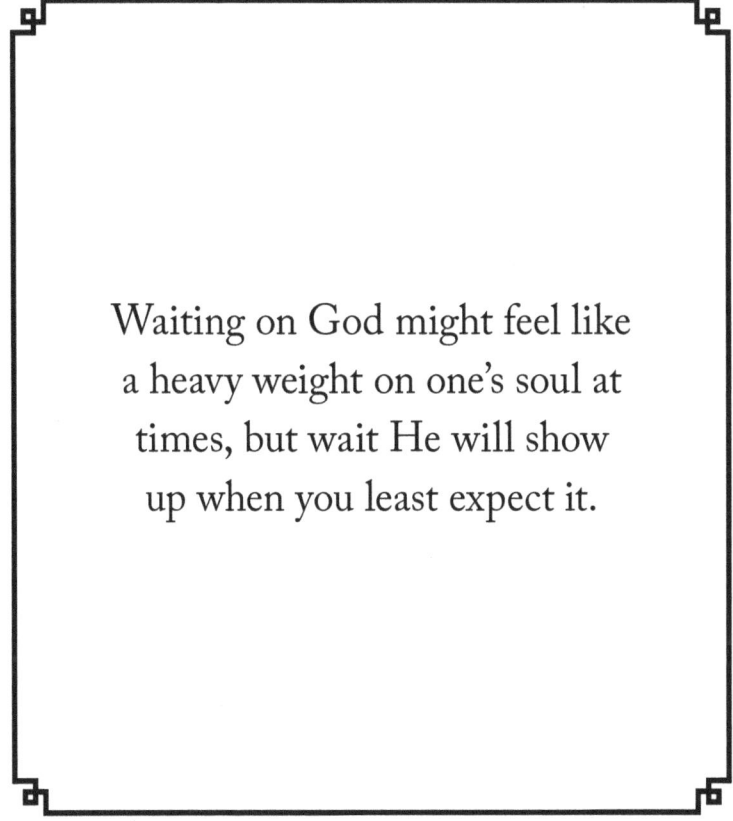

Waiting on God might feel like a heavy weight on one's soul at times, but wait He will show up when you least expect it.

If one lets his light go dim, his
world will no longer be lit.

Time does not run out on ideas, but time could run out before implementation.

Don't let the past control you...
don't let the bad times win.

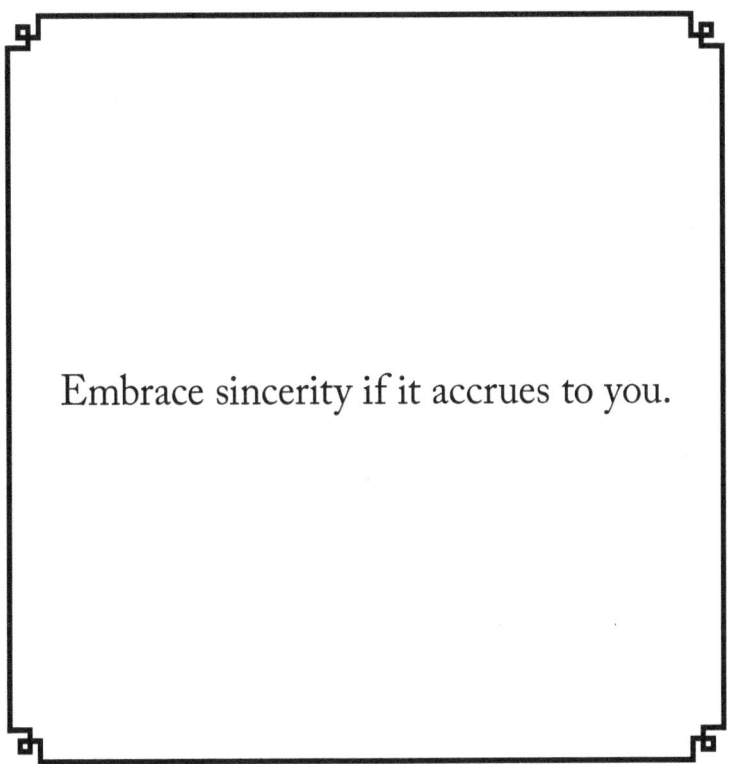

Embrace sincerity if it accrues to you.

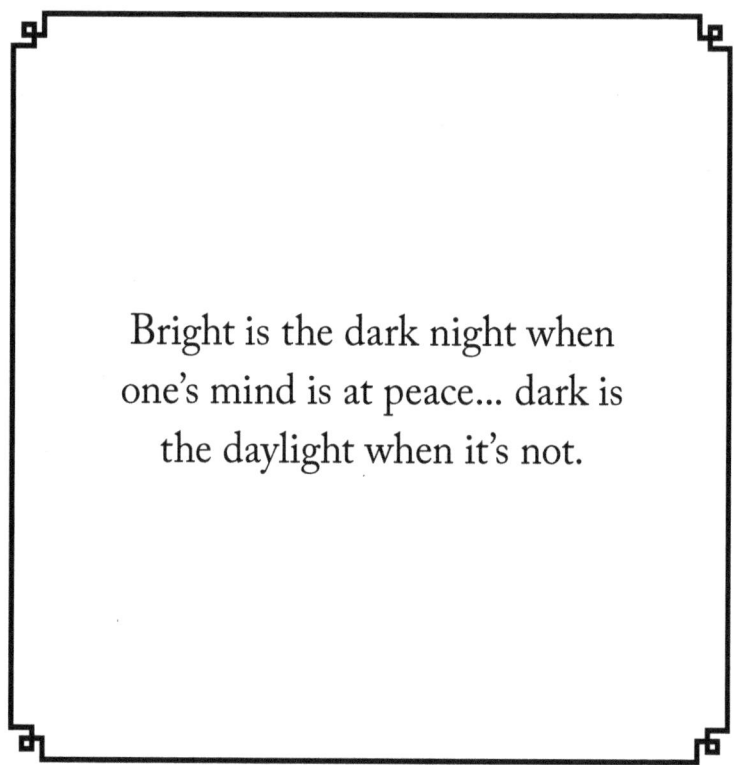

Bright is the dark night when
one's mind is at peace... dark is
the daylight when it's not.

It's okay for shiny objects to evoke curiosity in the passerby, but closer inspection can reveal how valueless those objects could really be. The true worth of a thing quite often has nothing to do with whether that thing has a shine or not.

Keep all tools handy... there's
much work yet to be done.

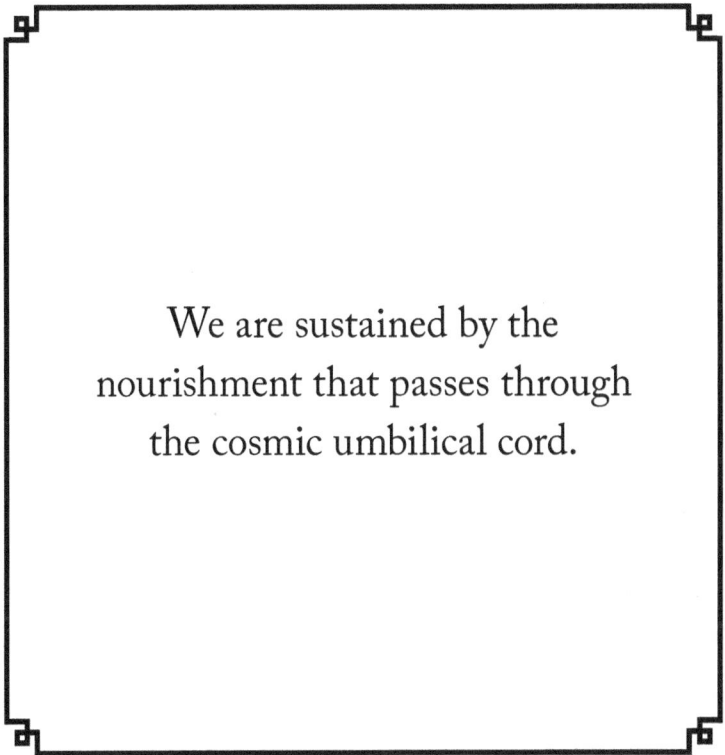

We are sustained by the
nourishment that passes through
the cosmic umbilical cord.

To wrestle with angels is
to seal your defeat.

God in his wisdom has sentenced
us all to life... to live life... but
some through their actions
have chosen to live death.

Composting the debris of
your life creates fertile soil
for parasites to grow.

The indistinguishable is a syndrome of symptoms that are individually distinguishable from each other... look deeper to explore each component part.

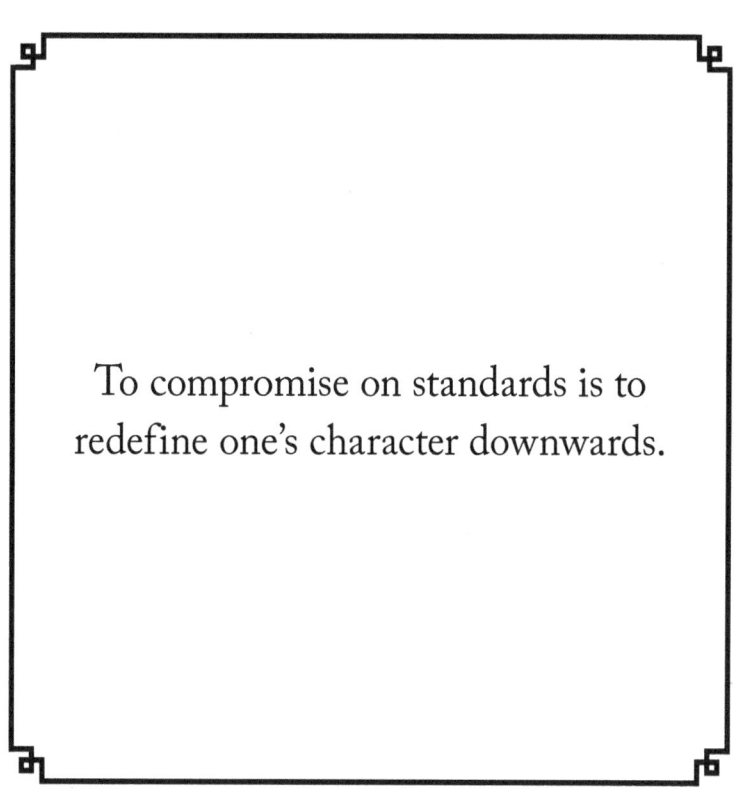

To compromise on standards is to redefine one's character downwards.

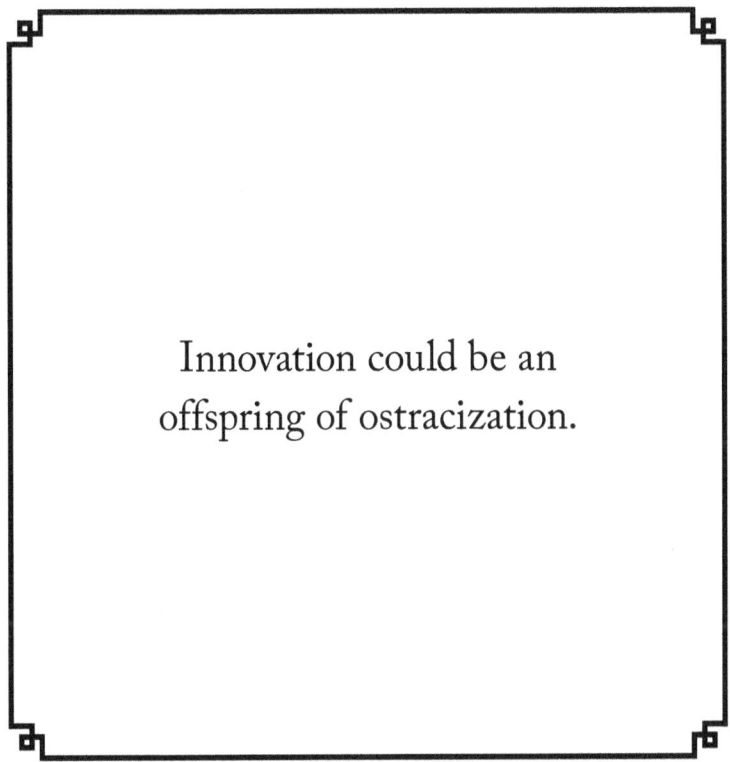

Innovation could be an
offspring of ostracization.

If it comes to the point where one feels as if he is marooned on an uninhabited island, one of his options is to lay claim to the island and have dominion over it.

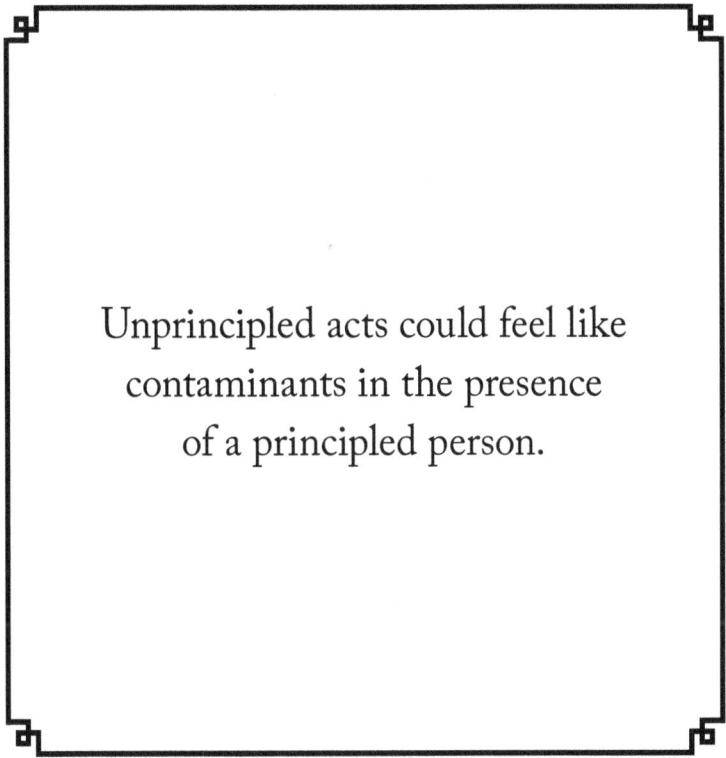

Unprincipled acts could feel like
contaminants in the presence
of a principled person.

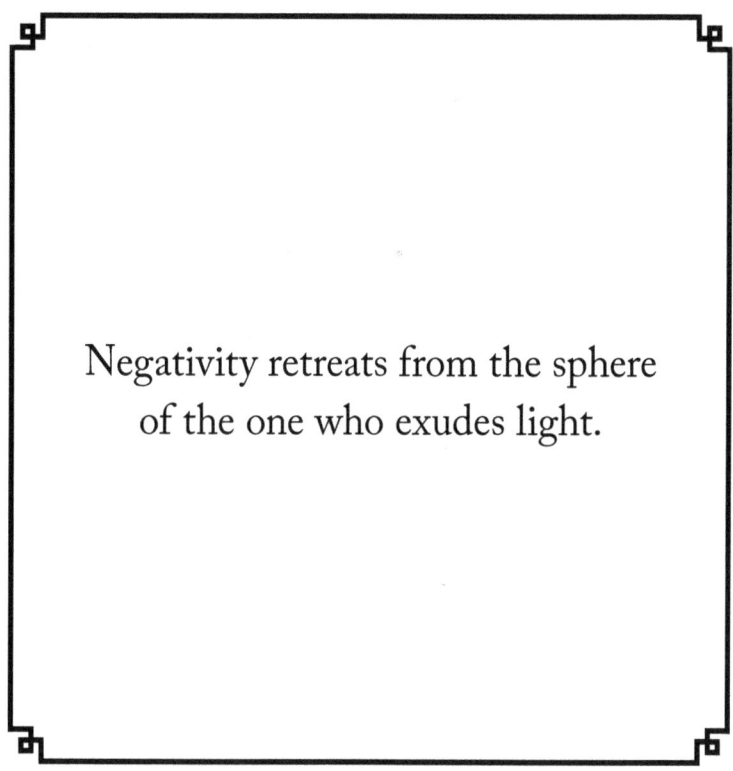

Negativity retreats from the sphere of the one who exudes light.

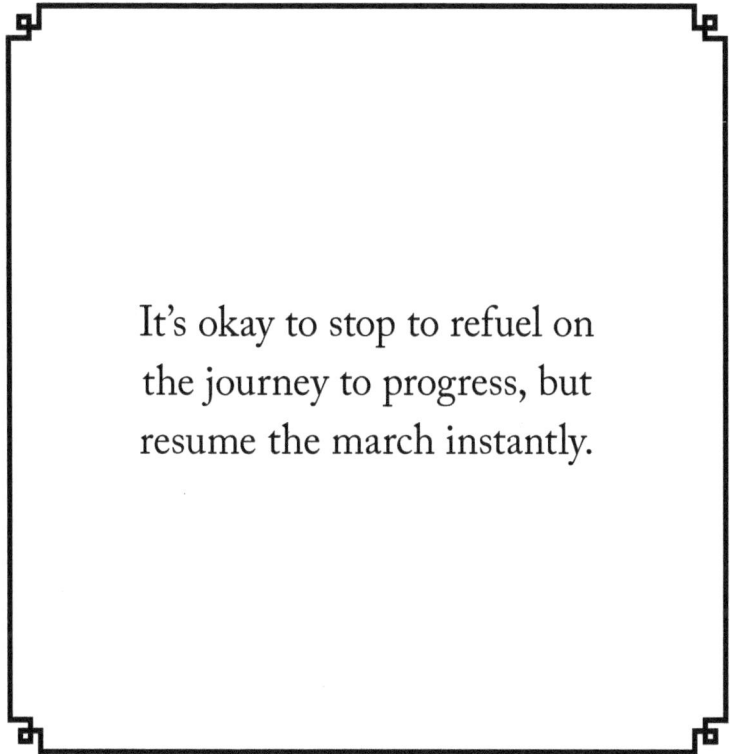

It's okay to stop to refuel on the journey to progress, but resume the march instantly.

People sometimes insist on searching for things that are not lost.

Once you make it to the
border of a new life lesson,
don't linger, step across.

One should be a spendthrift when it comes to emotional expenditure for too often that expense falls under the heading of discretionary spending.

Either one finds the missing piece
or it will find him... it simply
cannot remain missing forever.

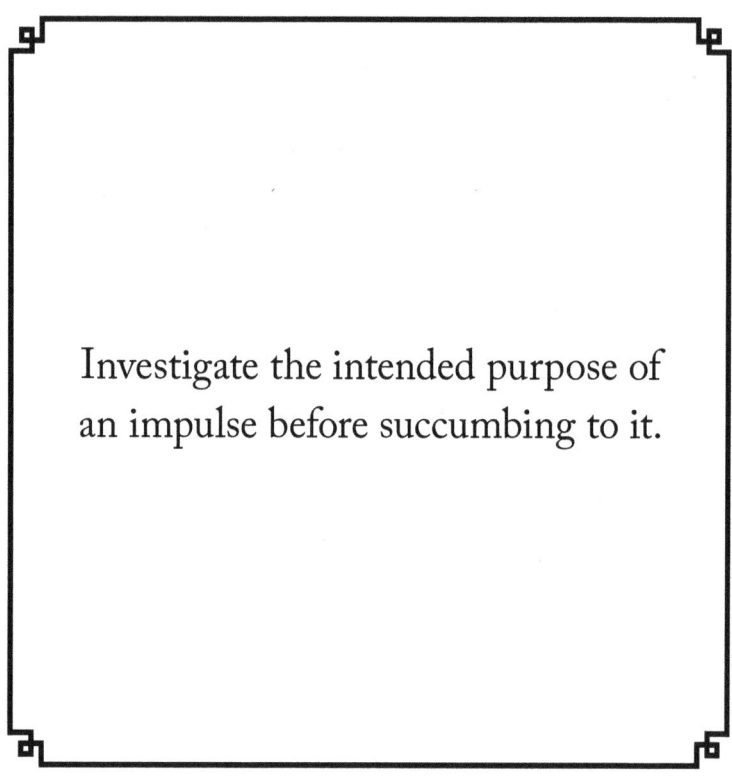

Investigate the intended purpose of an impulse before succumbing to it.

Staircases go up and down and if one finds himself in the middle of the stairs dizzied and confused by the whirling motion of his circumstances, he should pause and compose himself before taking the next step.

Having a hammer doesn't
make one a builder.

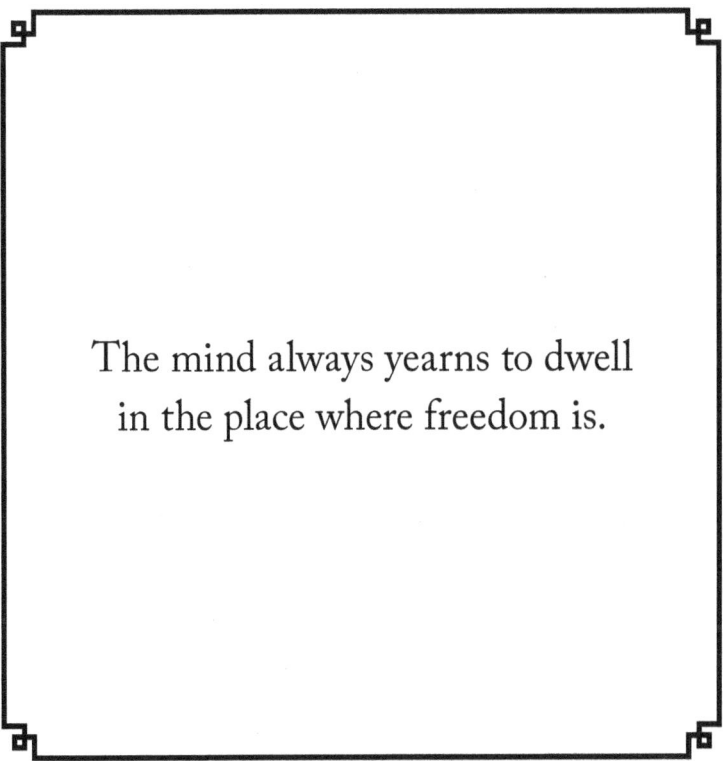

The mind always yearns to dwell
in the place where freedom is.

There is a Better You

Life presents in many different forms, and there are endless ways of evaluating circumstances and defining experiences. This is the stuff that has given rise to a parade of experts and their respective disciplines. There is an 'ist' for just about everything. Mental health therapists, psychiatrists, and psychologists endeavor to bring clarity and find ways for people to face their mental and psychological challenges and overcome them. In essence therapists help people to take control of their lives by facilitating their clients to take away the power from whatever the thing is that is holding them captive. An increasing number of people are making use of these services as awareness grows and it becomes more apparent that stigmatization no longer has to subject people to a life of lonely struggle when expert help is available. One should not think of it as taboo to enlist the help of such experts when it is clearly indicated that the fight you have been having between yourself and your internal nemeses would not be won without an ally on your side. If you think that people will speak derogatively of you saying that you are going to a 'shrink', then do not pay them any mind. The mere fact that they are choosing to look down upon you for choosing to untangle your psychological knots is an indication that they, with their unstudied, simplistic selves, need to have some mental detoxing done upon them. The people who make the choice to get help often do so after a prolonged effort to cope with their circumstances by themselves, and the pain that comes along with this process cannot be underestimated. This puts the individual at the mercy of her circumstances, and it takes a strong desire to change by rejecting the belief that this is the card she was dealt and must play for the rest of her life. Most people want to feel in control of their lives, so it is not a happy place to be when one has to appear solid on the outside while being a blob of mushy chaos on the inside. Professional help aside, some situations can be addressed by taking the time to make a self- discovery. This process can be set in motion through the deliberate decision to realign one's thinking from that of feeling self-pity to one of imagining a life without the hurt. In no way will I minimize the trauma of abuse and the impact it could have on self-esteem, especially if the abuse involved the forced disintegration of youthful innocence, but the victim's default position should be a dedication to working to overcome such impact. Everyone deserves to pursue happiness, but dragging heavy burdens behind you will make it so much more difficult, if not near-impossible, to reach that goal. Whereas this, realistically, could be easier said than done, the point is that it can be done, it has been done, and it needs to be done. If the trauma is derived from relationship drama, as adults, people should realize that their partners, just as they, have the ability to make choices and will make choices they perceive to be in their own best interest even if it leaves one partner devastated. If you are the devastated partner, you need to know that it is reasonable to feel that sense of betrayal or loss, but it is not productive to live in that mental space for a prolonged length of time. This will only bring you more pain, more loss, and more devastation even as your ex-partner is having the opposite reaction. Always believe that you are worthy, and awesome, and valuable; and no one, not even someone whom you were/are emotionally attached to, could prevent you from being the best person that you could be. Let it go! Let him go! You would never have been your best self in a climate of drama anyway. Count his departure as a blessing. What might seem to be loneliness is actually the uninterrupted, drama-free space God has provided for you to connect with your spirit. And none of this would be possible in a situation of muddled distractions. The best of you is yet to be revealed. Stop preventing it from surfacing!

"Finding the Balance." – S. Barrock

Clutter is a retardant to progress.

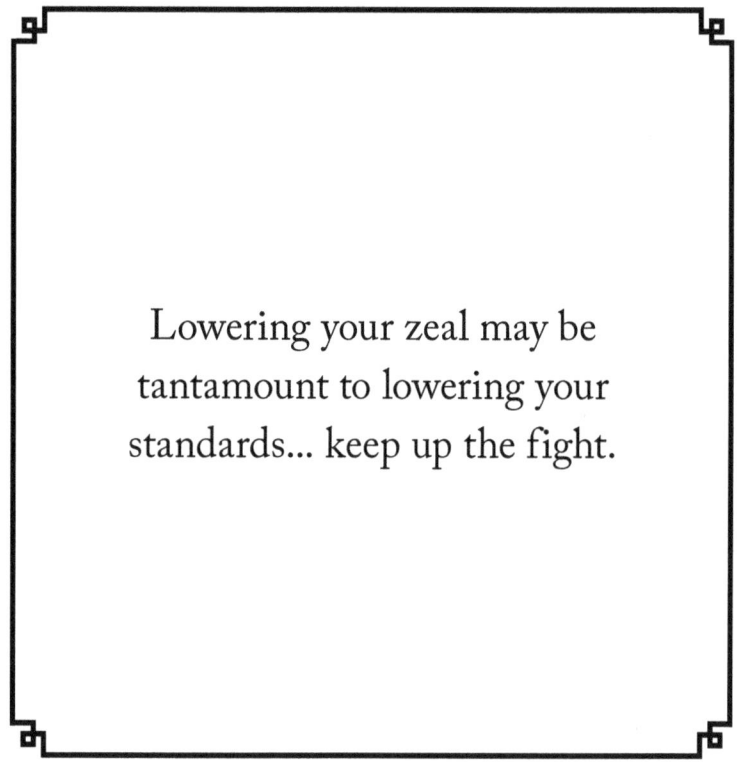

Lowering your zeal may be tantamount to lowering your standards... keep up the fight.

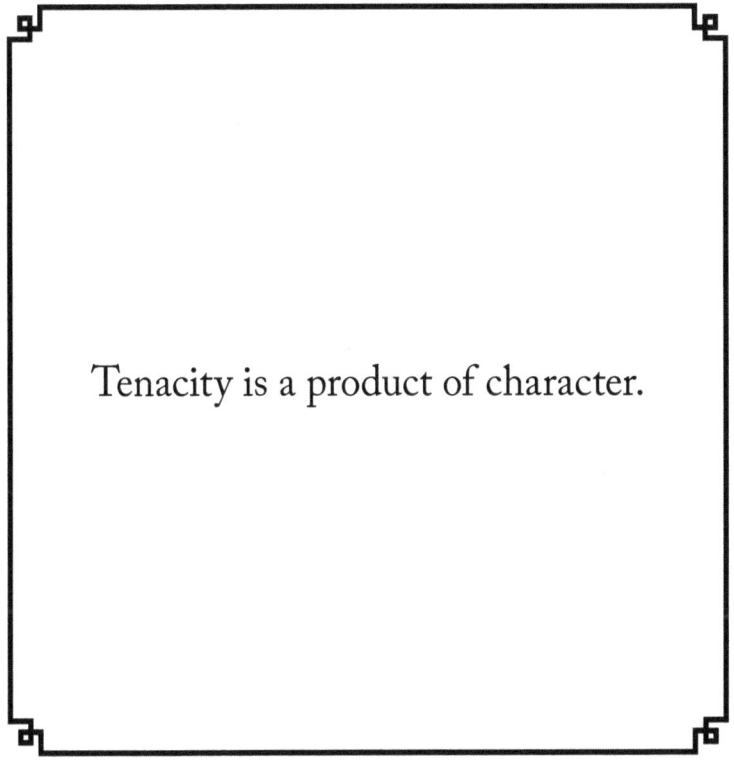

Tenacity is a product of character.

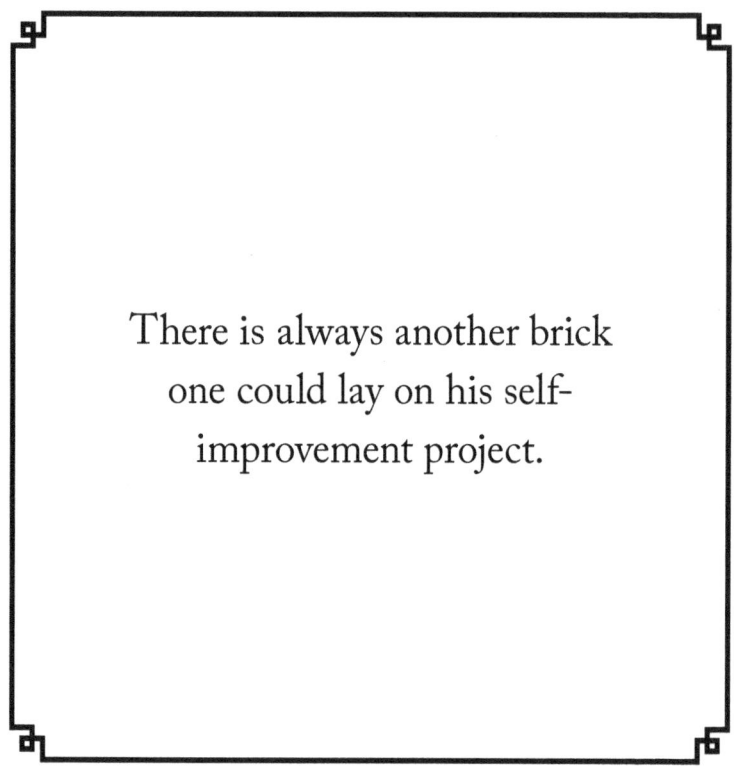

There is always another brick one could lay on his self-improvement project.

If drama somehow makes it to
your guest list, disinvite it.

Just care about somebody...
it's not complicated.

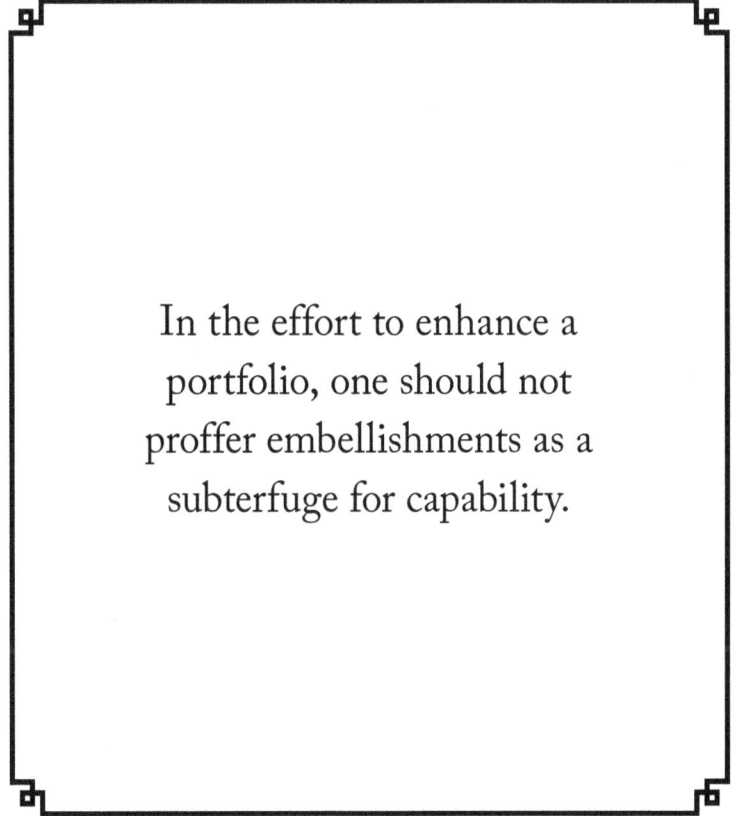

In the effort to enhance a portfolio, one should not proffer embellishments as a subterfuge for capability.

The mental space one provides
for new content should be
free of unwanted material.

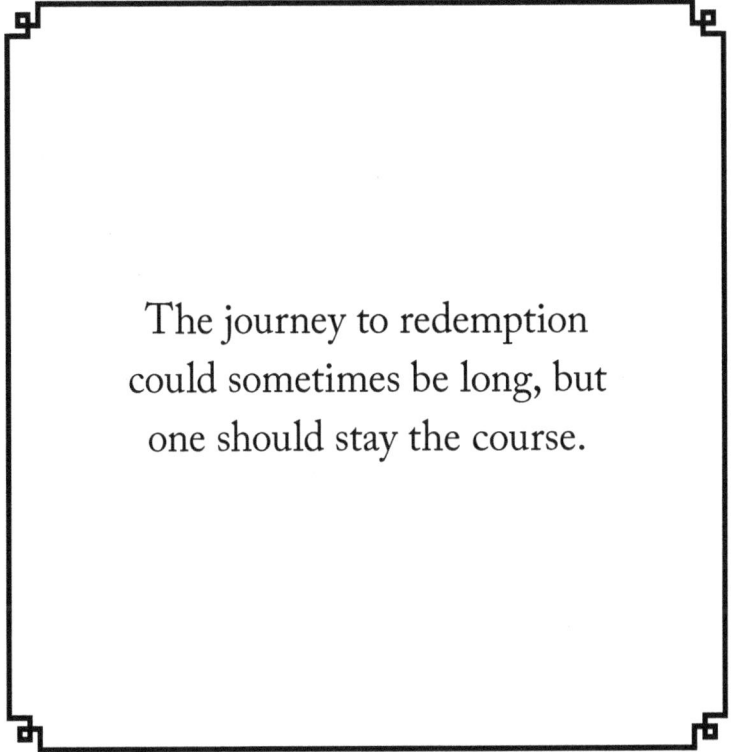

The journey to redemption
could sometimes be long, but
one should stay the course.

It's not ethical to claim to possess exceptional eyesight when the day itself is unusually clear.

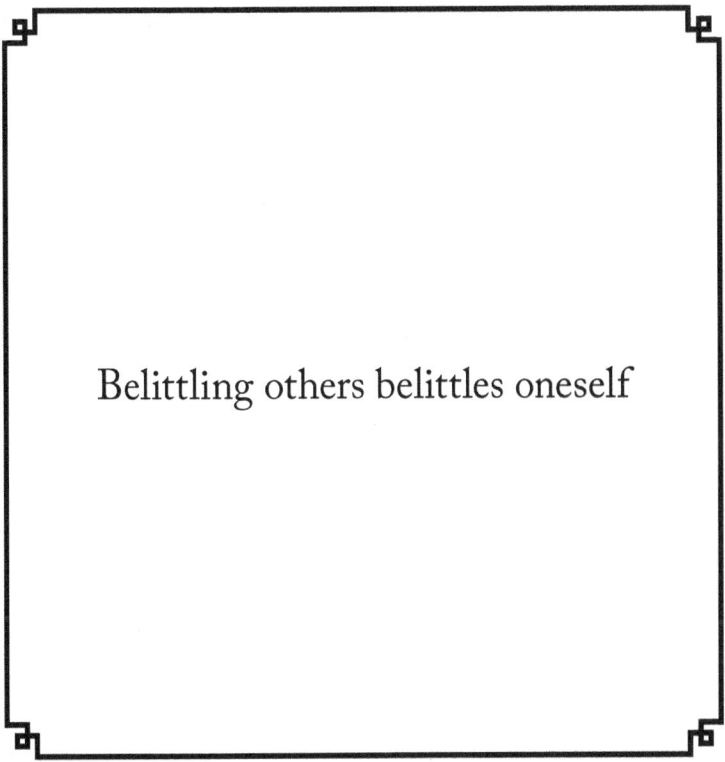

Belittling others belittles oneself

Remediate when you mess up

Try to make a new discovery each day

Appreciate then celebrate

Some circumstances require
you to go into attack mode

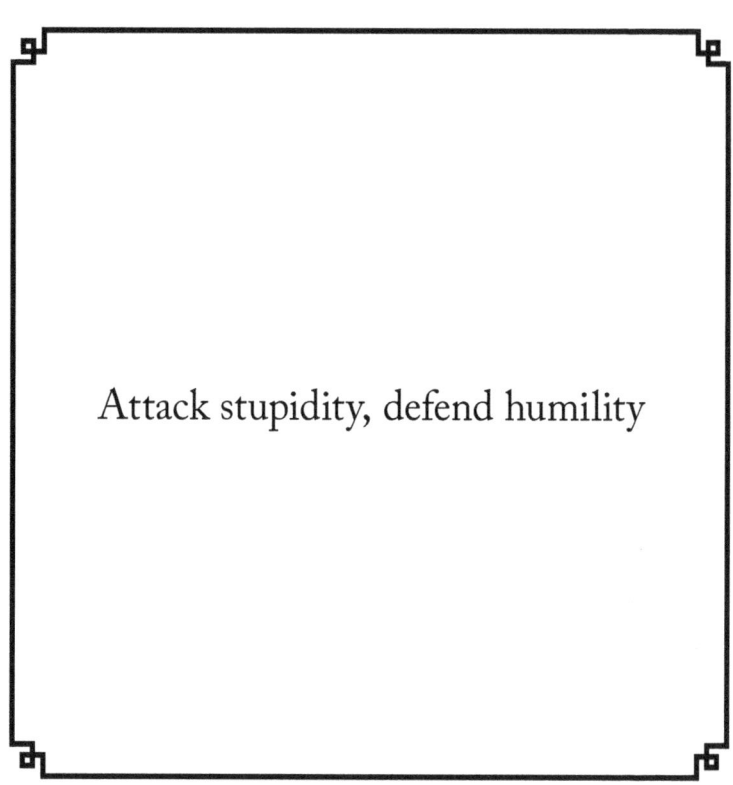

Attack stupidity, defend humility

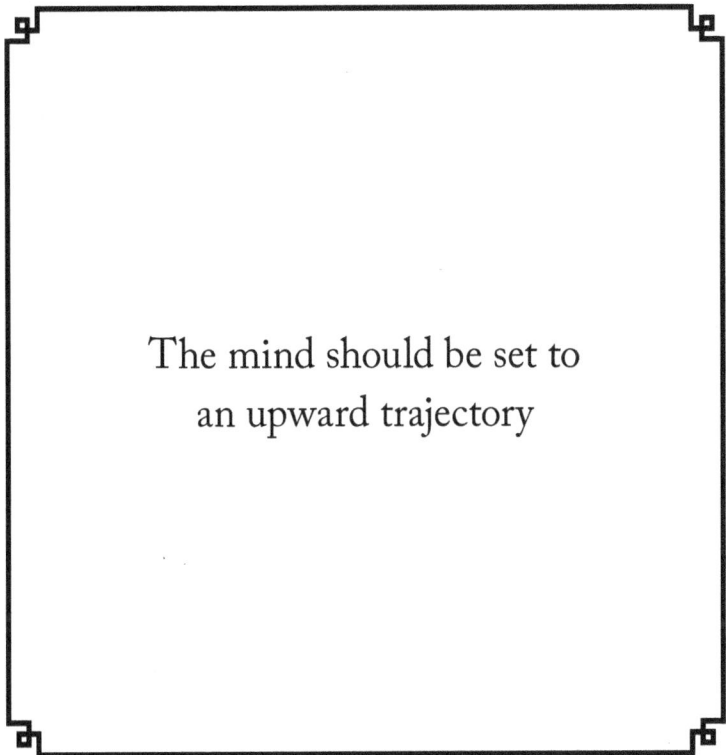

The mind should be set to
an upward trajectory

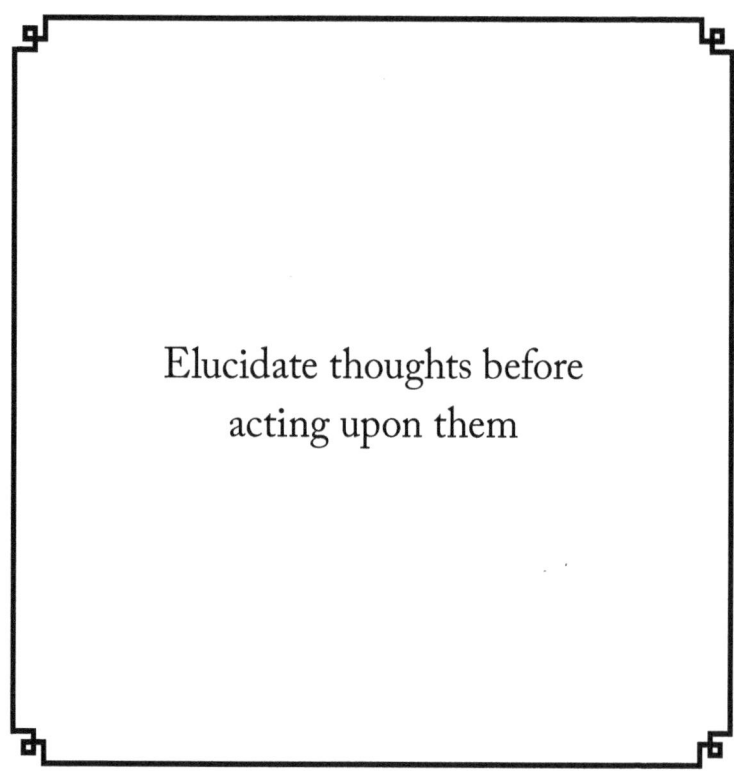

Elucidate thoughts before
acting upon them

Shine a bright light upon
an obscure target

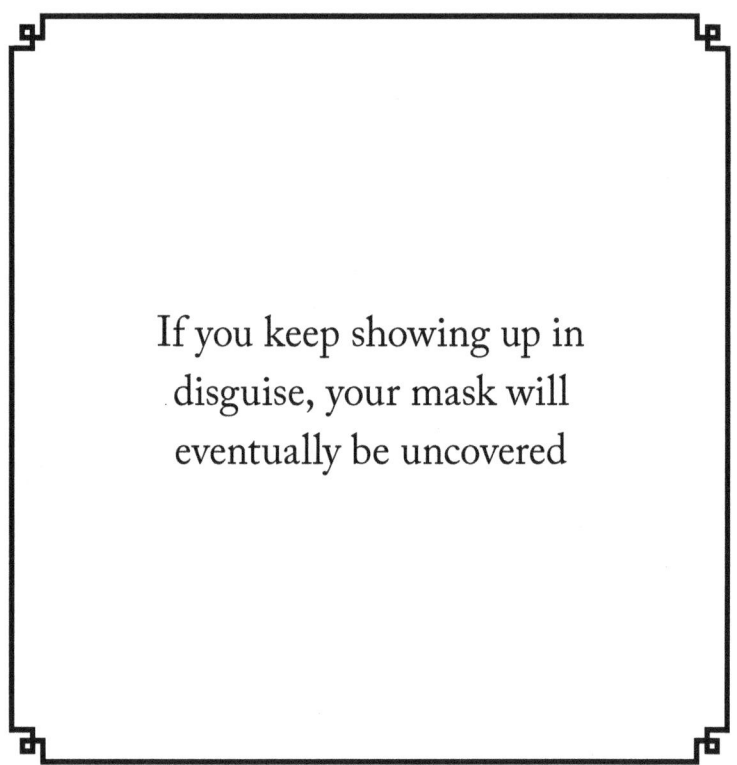

If you keep showing up in
disguise, your mask will
eventually be uncovered

Seek just compensation;
give just compensation

Always look for opportunities
to perturb the status quo

Overlay goodness with meekness

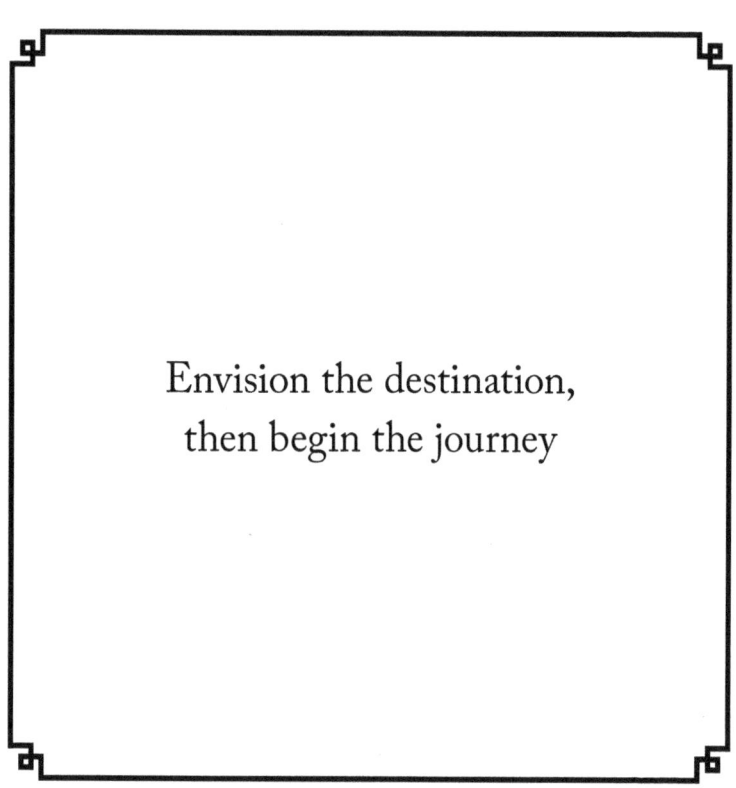

Envision the destination,
then begin the journey

Music penetrates the soul

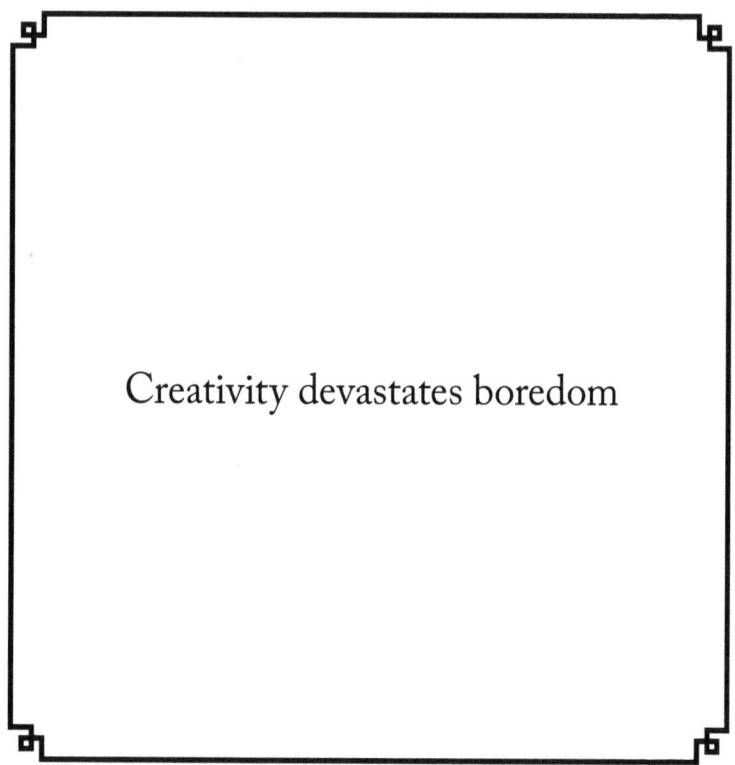

Creativity devastates boredom

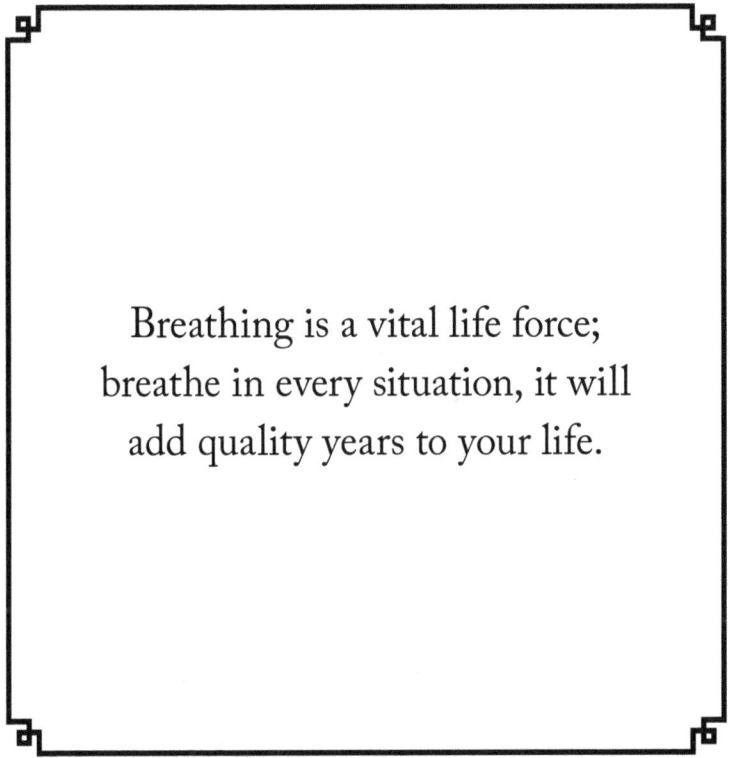

Breathing is a vital life force; breathe in every situation, it will add quality years to your life.

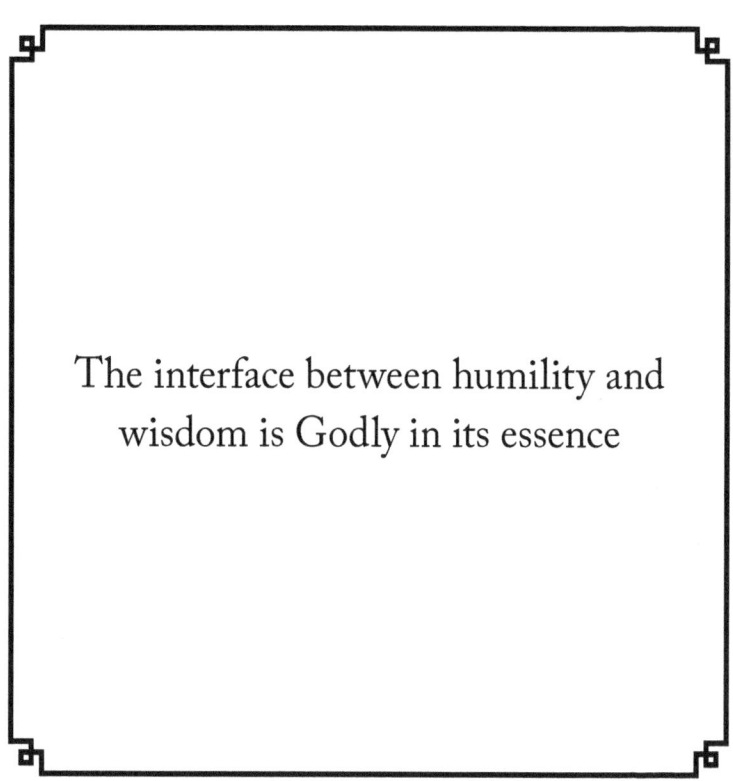

The interface between humility and
wisdom is Godly in its essence

A meal might look appealing and smell enticing, but is it digestible?

Helping someone in need
should be effortless

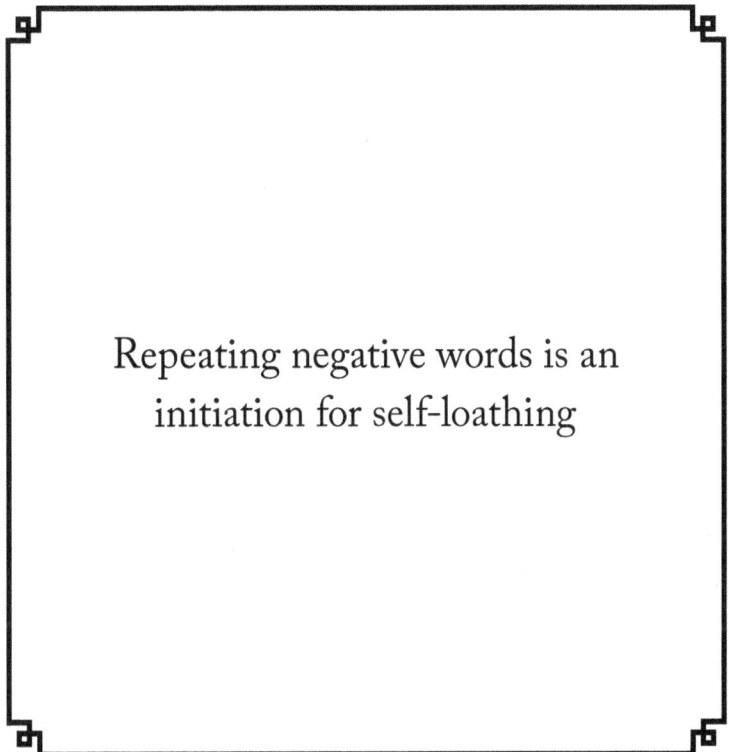

Repeating negative words is an
initiation for self-loathing

Invest time into efforts that
have positive deliverables

Indulge in happiness

Stop Intercepting Your Blessings

How many times have you wondered why the arrival of your blessings seems excessively prolonged? This is not an unusual topic of speculation because one's desire to move from one stage in life to a better, more comfortable stage in life is often combined with a measure of anxiety. Anxiety expressed in the right proportion is understandable, but when it becomes all- consuming, it presents as a negative, and prevents a person from clearing the mental and psychological channel leading from the storehouse of the blessing to the point of manifestation in that person's life. I would wager that more, not fewer of us have a wish to be in a different place than the one we are in now. There are missing pieces somewhere out there that would close the circle for us and bring us the kind of contentment we seek. Those missing pieces could represent needs that are not being met currently: financial, emotional, spiritual, physical, social, educational among others. Once those needs are met, we might consider ourselves blessed. The timeline between the desires and the fulfillment or satisfaction of these desires vary from person to person just as the desires themselves vary from person to person. All things being equal, the process from desire to manifestation is sometimes controllable, and a reasonable expectation of a timeline is permissible. If a person desires to be an automobile mechanic for example, he knows that he has to put in the time to train and become proficient at that trade. So too is anyone pursuing whatever the vocation of his choice might be. Working hard to obtain a college degree could feel like a blessing received when graduation day arrives. The above are examples of blessings wrapped up in achievements and regularly position an individual to advance in his desired field. This process can help such a person quantify his potential for material success.

There are many people who cannot declare a vocation or particular industrial skill, but no one is excluded as a prospect for the receipt of a blessing. Most everyone is likely working to achieve something in life; however mundane or limited this might appear on the surface. Contentment does not look the same way to everyone, and it only matters that a heart is lifted a level above where it was the day before. There are other kinds of blessings, not quantifiable or controllable, that arrive outside of our capacity to anticipate or control them. These are transcendent phenomena at work in the spiritual realm. While we cannot control how and when they arrive in our lives, the way we choose to live situate us to receive these blessings. It was the Apostle Paul who advised us that our transformation comes from the renewing of our minds. This was true then and it is true now. Real achievement goes beyond material gain. As with anything material, it can be fleeting and subject the possessor to the power of his possessions. Incidentally, any power the material possession has over its owner is the one handed over to it by the owner himself. A new way of thinking means a new way of viewing the world, a new way of defining and dealing with challenges, and a new pattern and feel of the vibrations you transmit to the world. This necessarily means that some people will want to embrace you even more while others will fell estranged in your presence and eventually change course. This change has more to do with those people than it has to do with you. Their reaction to the new you has a direct relationship to the state of readiness of their minds and their current capacity to withstand the increased luminosity of your light. There is a noticeable outward glow associated with the one who is undergoing a renewal of her mind, and an inner lightness spawned by the peace that comes with it. Transcendent blessings will normally follow the path back to the source of transmission of spiritually-pure vibrations, and they arrive at their own time and choosing. They may be deflected or halted if the intended receiver fails to maintain her transcendent mental posture and allows old, useless issues that existed before the renewal of her mind, to infiltrate and derail the blessing before it reaches her. She should live a life high on vigilance and low on anxiety.

"Turbulent patches in our lives are bound by space and time but only if we resolve to sail past them in pursuit of our liberation." - S. Barrock

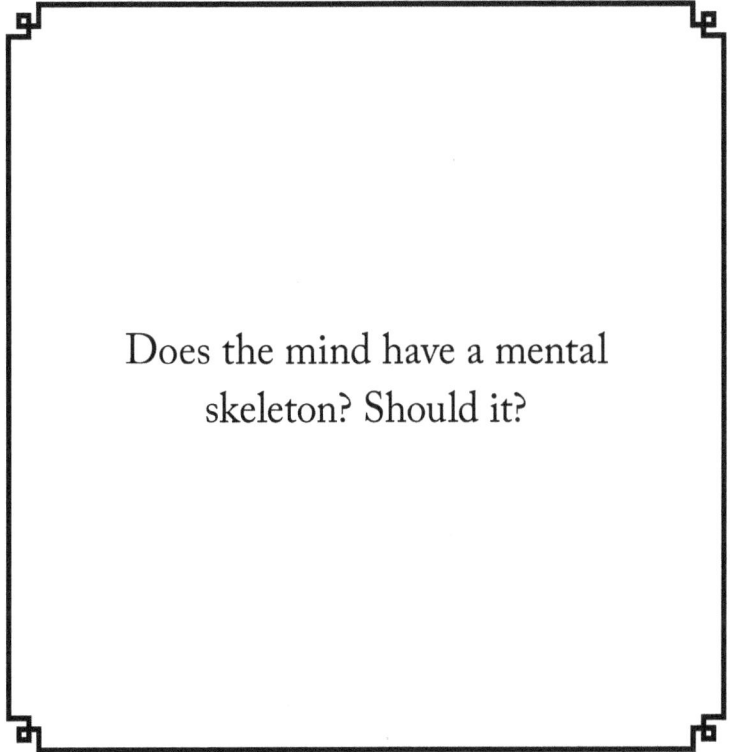

Does the mind have a mental
skeleton? Should it?

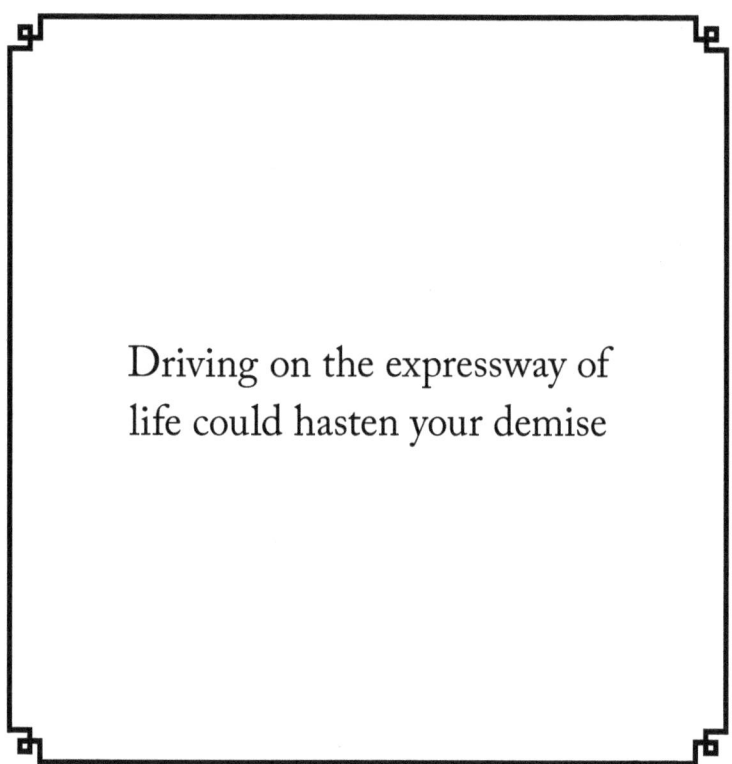

Driving on the expressway of
life could hasten your demise

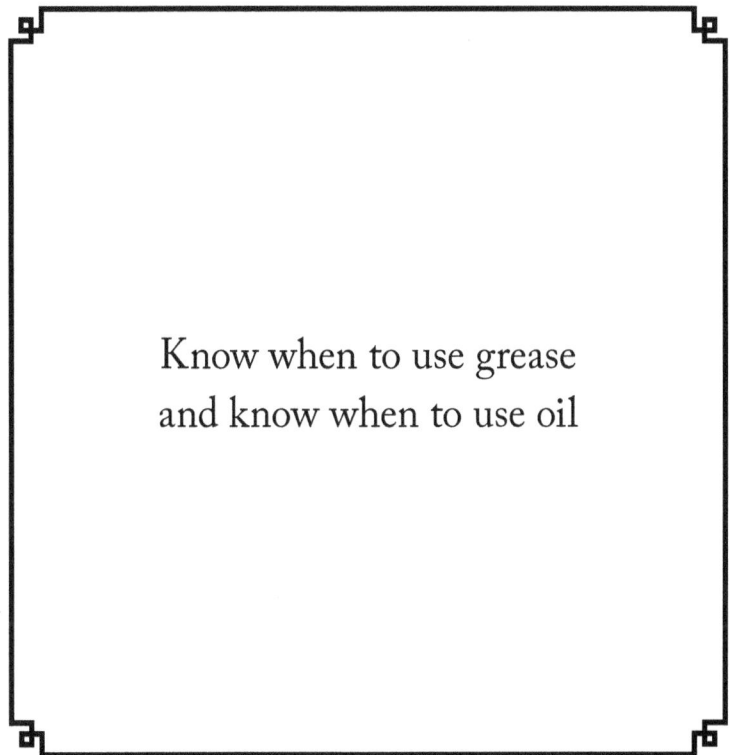

Know when to use grease
and know when to use oil

Repair damages that are repairable
otherwise replace the whole unit

Place limits where limits
are indicated

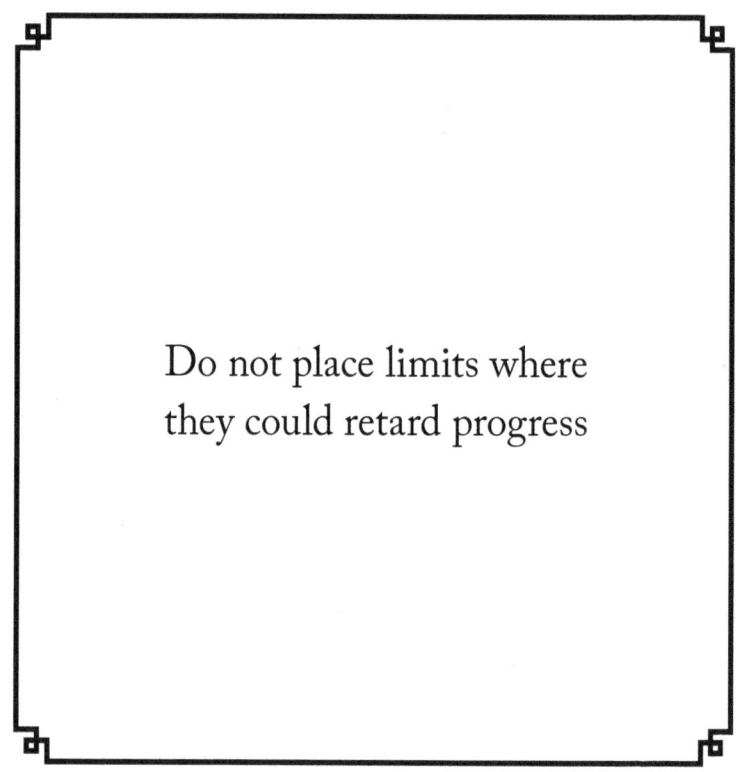

Do not place limits where
they could retard progress

Label yourself as worthy,
capable, and awesome

Reject labels that others
place on you

Your battles are yours to fight

Breathe slowly, deeply
and purposefully

Fill the heart with compassion

Hard times do not target people;
hard time cannot think

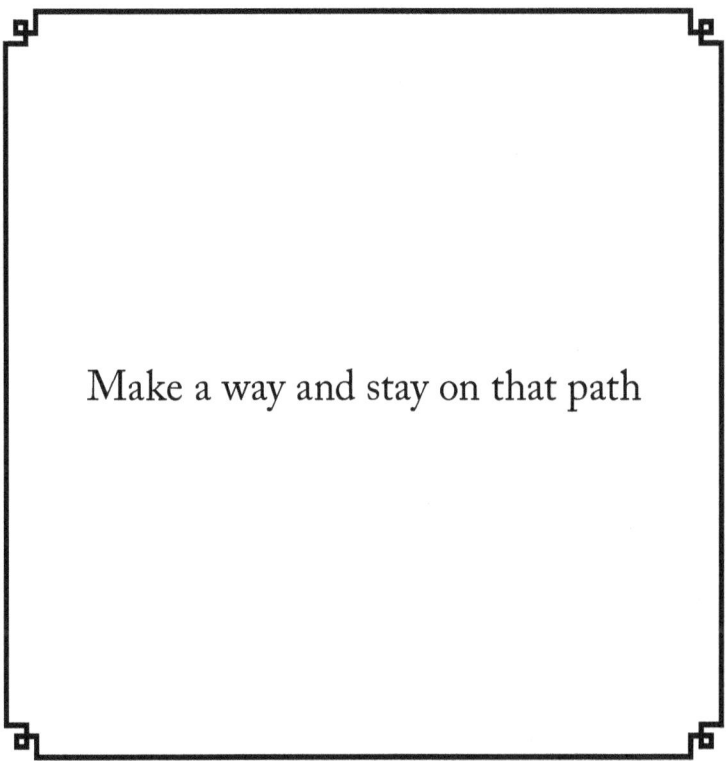

Make a way and stay on that path

It's hard to unsee the seen

Love the unloved

Don't carry burdens;
put them down

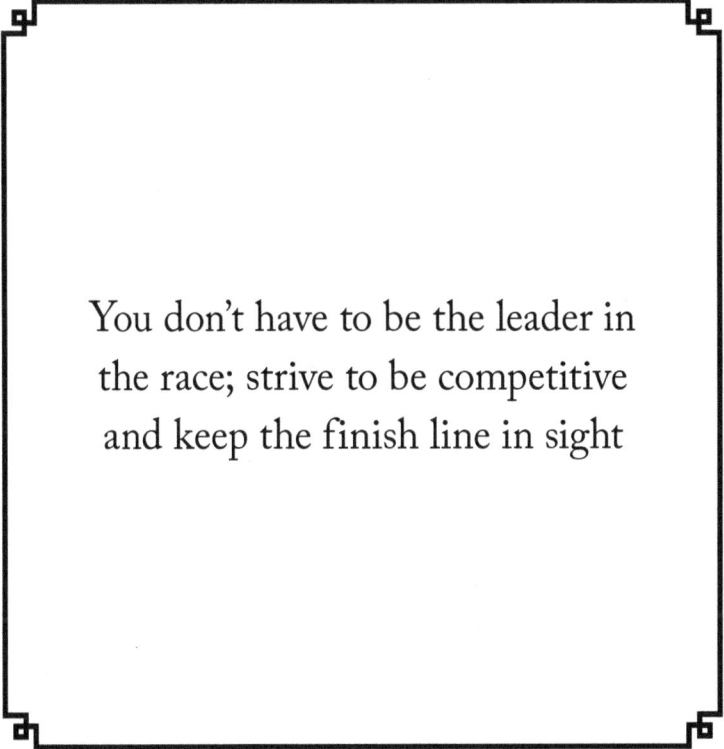

You don't have to be the leader in the race; strive to be competitive and keep the finish line in sight

When you reach the top, where else can you go? Help others up.

Overloading the mind is like
over roasting a turkey; enjoyment
dwindles with each extra unit of heat

Wish it for others if you
would wish it for yourself

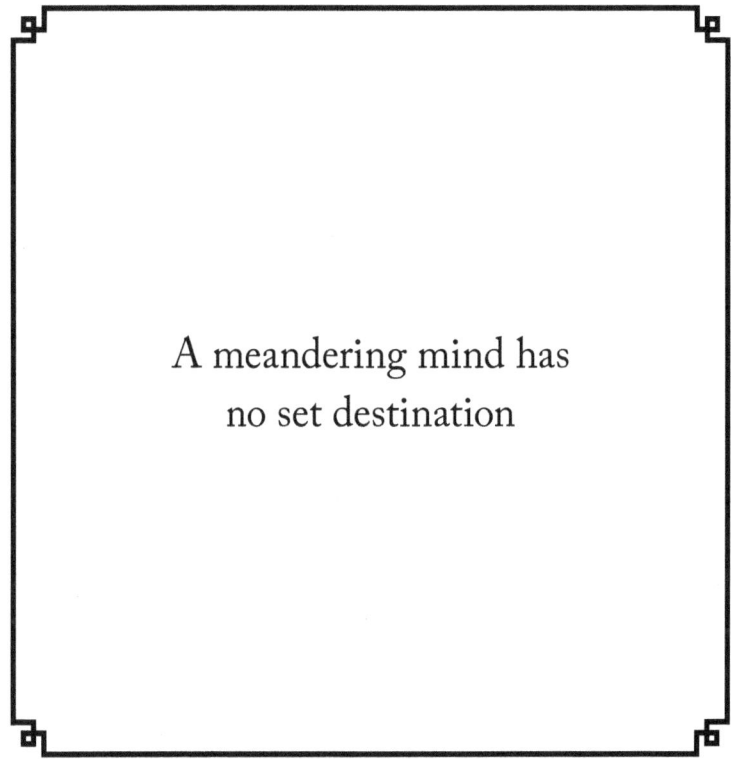

A meandering mind has
no set destination

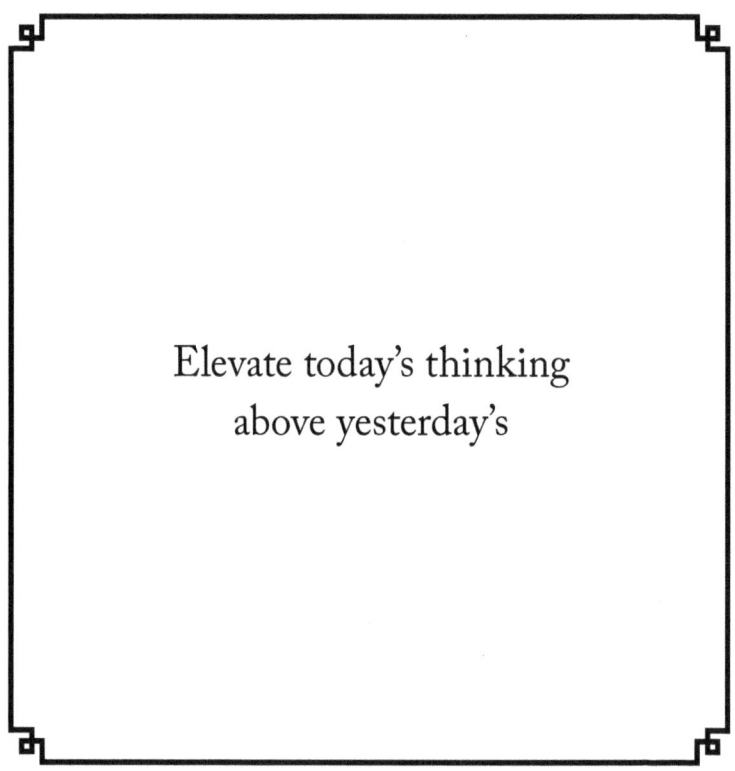

Elevate today's thinking
above yesterday's

A clearer vision is in juxtaposition
to an open mind

Don't stop working until
the task is completed

Truth is a good conscience booster

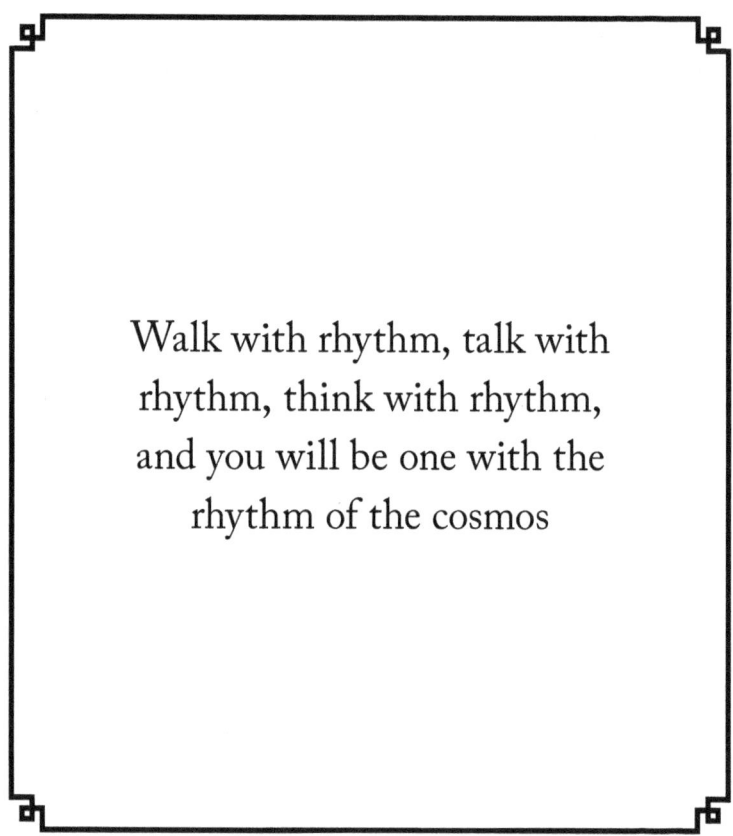

Walk with rhythm, talk with rhythm, think with rhythm, and you will be one with the rhythm of the cosmos

Your expectations will be
manifested with time

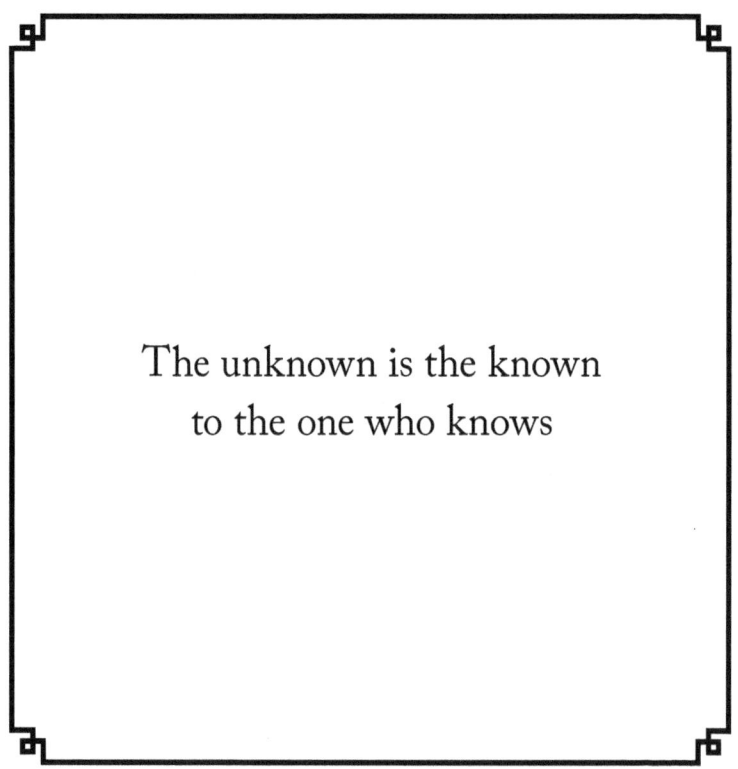

The unknown is the known
to the one who knows

Sometimes to know a little
is to know too much

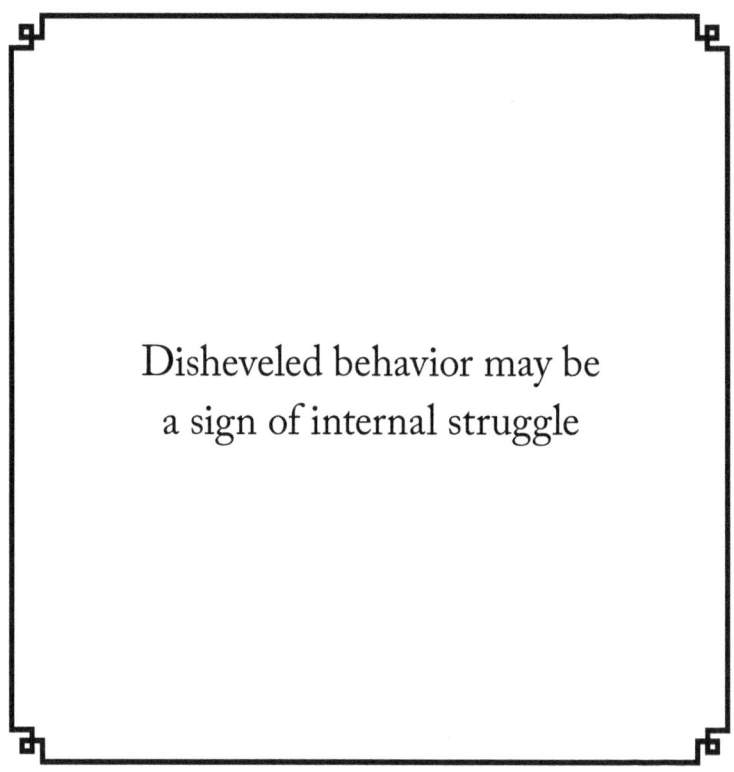

Disheveled behavior may be
a sign of internal struggle

Stop hanging off the edges of life

Stop sleeping on the ledge of life

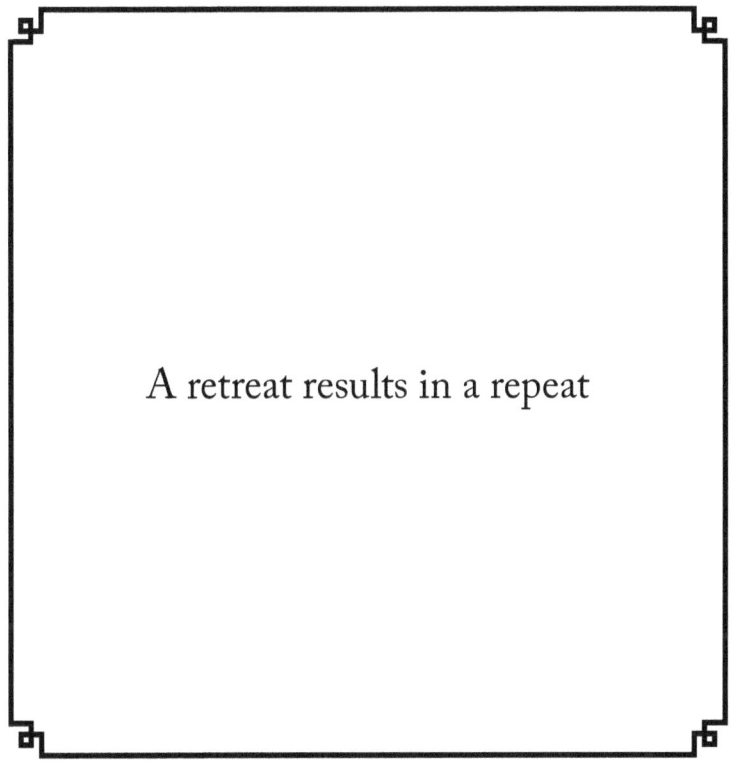

A retreat results in a repeat

Is Gratefulness the Default Position of Your Heart?

In the deepest part of your being you are convinced that you have been doing everything possible to remain on a progressive track while trying to make a contribution to the betterment of yourself and the world around you. You do this through posting positive messages on social media, reaching out to friends and acquaintances through private messaging, in-person interactions, and making and receiving calls to help others work their way out of some emotional or mental maze they might find themselves in. If you are so blessed as to be chosen for a role like this, then you should allow gratefulness to be the default position of your heart. Be grateful that God has seen something in you that you may not have even seen in yourself. And if this is the case, there is no need to think about the size or factor of difficulty associated with the task. It is sufficient to be confident that the giver of the task will guide you through every facet of the process. People will begin to notice that yours is a reliable place of resort when they need guidance or simply a listening ear to help them figure out their current circumstances and plot a course for a more gratifying future. And so they come without hesitation! They come with a mission to utilize your kindness and sincere desire to lift them up. After a while, they leave with a sense of accomplishment and a renewed orientation towards life. Most leave without looking back, but others reflect with a sense of gratitude and state their appreciation for your involvement in their voyage. The people in the latter group are the ones who understand that thankfulness is a quality proximate to godliness, and they are likely to be the ones to maintain the sanctification derived from their interaction with you. Whereas it may be true that some among those who did not look back are choosing to keep their gratitude in the quiet places of their hearts, it is a better bet for them to proclaim their redemption to the world. In so doing, they would provide a testimony that could inspire others to find their way through their own labyrinths in life. And those same people who benefited in the first place could become practitioners of the parallel process that initially liberated them. A well-developed sense of awareness will not estrange a person from the idea that life is cyclical in its essence and attitudes and behaviors are merely recycled through generations. Many of us would have heard about the story of the ten lepers who were cleansed but only 'one' made the decision to give thanks for his cleansing. The question of the 'nine' who did not do likewise is still in existence in both a practical and figurative sense today. We do not do ourselves any favors when we choose to hoard our blessings rather than sharing them. It is a simple rule that the more you accumulate, the heavier the burden of responsibility you heap upon yourself, and before long your blessing could resemble a curse; you could be residing in the middle of a storm of clutter. Blessings are perishable if not maintained and utilized, and the more you share them, the more room you will make for other blessings to enter your life. Count them, proclaim them, and inspire others by them. We run into many 'Nines' in our daily encounters, but they have a role to play as well.

'Nines' can teach us how not to respond when someone helps us to experience a new vision or a new outlook on life. Make the choice to be a 'One'. Once again, let gratefulness be the default position of your heart and proclaim it to be so.

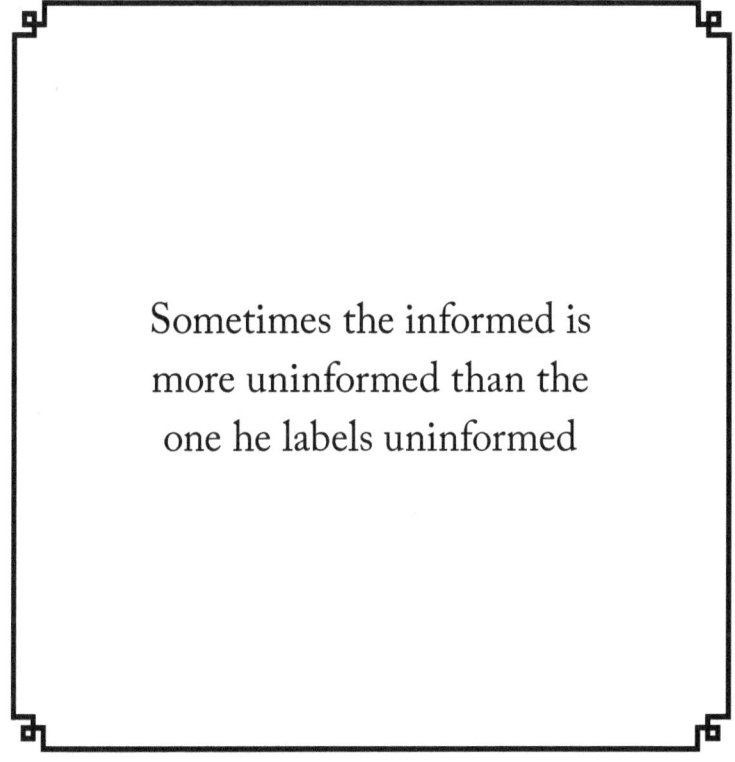

Sometimes the informed is more uninformed than the one he labels uninformed

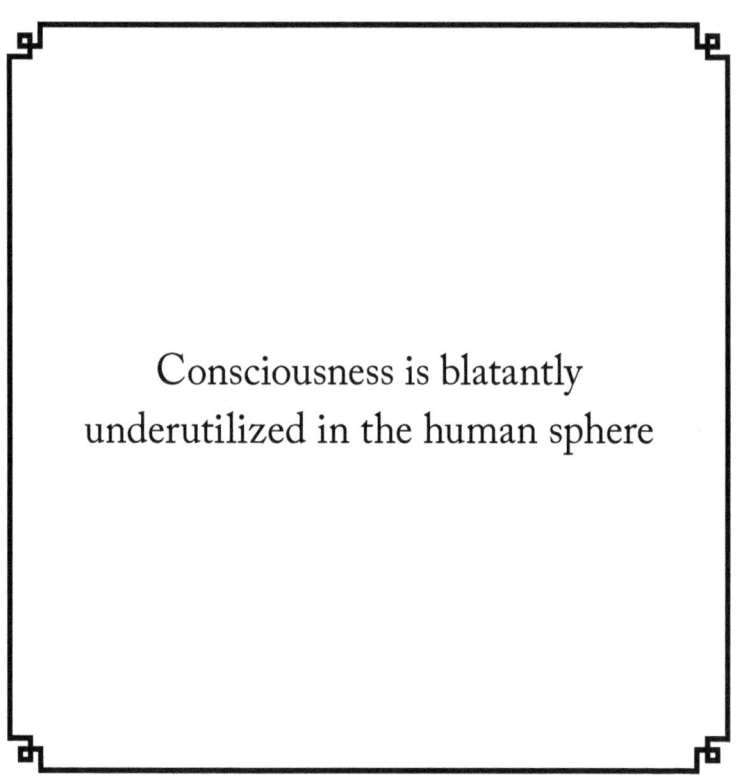

Consciousness is blatantly
underutilized in the human sphere

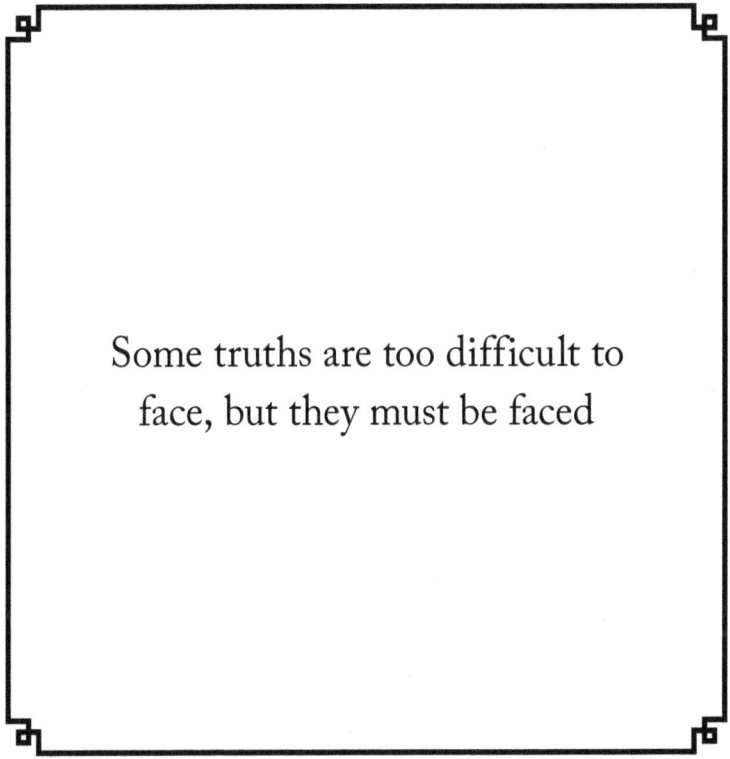

Some truths are too difficult to face, but they must be faced

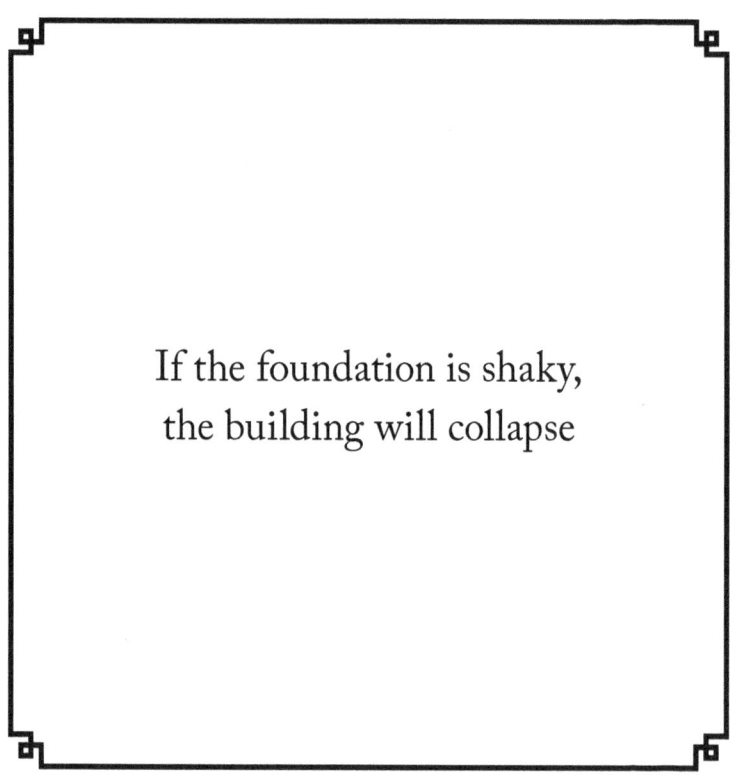

If the foundation is shaky,
the building will collapse

See yourself in others for we are all partakers in the cosmic commons

Just because something is unseen
doesn't mean it is not there.

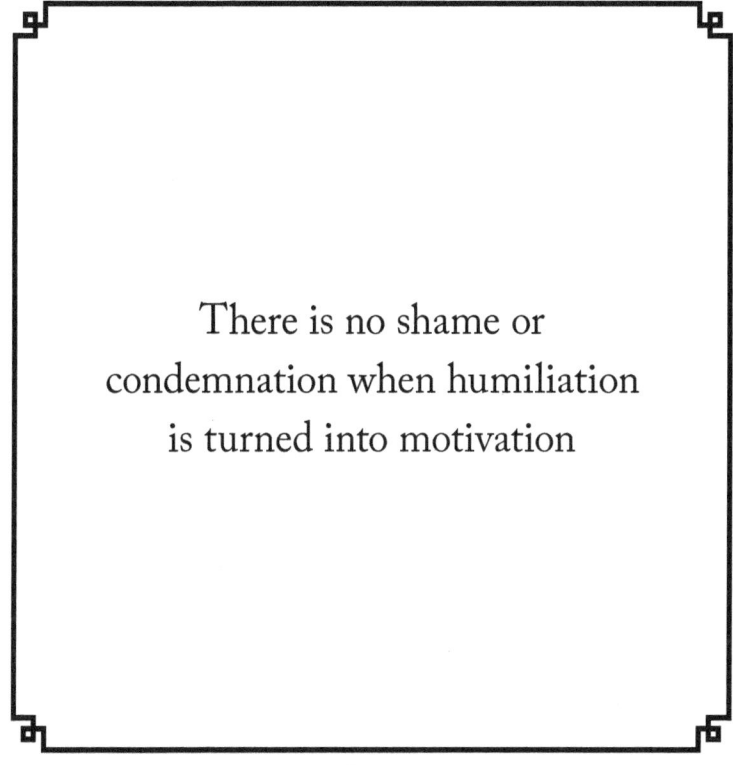

There is no shame or
condemnation when humiliation
is turned into motivation